STICKER NATION

THE BIG BOOK OF SUBVERSIVE STICKERS VOLUME 1

CREATED BY

SRINI KUMAR

disinformation®

D1294396

© 2006 Srini Kumar

Published by The Disinformation Company Ltd.
163 Third Avenue, Suite 108
New York, NY 10003
Tel.: +1.212.691.1605
Fax: +1.212.691.1606
www.disinfo.com

All rights reserved. No part of this book may be reproduced, stored in a database or other retrieval system, or transmitted in any form, by any means now existing or later discovered, including without limitation mechanical, electronic, photographic or otherwise, without the express prior written permission of the publisher.

Library of Congress Control Number: 2006921704

ISBN-13: 978-1-932857-28-3
ISBN-10: 1-932857-28-1

Printed in Thailand

10 9 8 7 6 5 4 3 2 1

Production Editor: Ralph Bernardo
Cover Design: Srini Kumar and Jacob Rosette

Distributed in the USA and Canada by:
Consortium Book Sales and Distribution
1045 Westgate Drive, Suite 90
St Paul, MN 55114
Toll Free: +1.800.283.3572 Local: +1.651.221.9035
Fax: +1.651.221.0124
www.cbsd.com

Distributed in the United Kingdom and Eire by:
Virgin Books
Thames Wharf Studios, Rainville Road
London W6 9HA
Tel.: +44.(0)20.7386.3300
Fax: +44.(0)20.7386.3360
E-Mail: sales@virgin-books.co.uk

Distributed in Australia by:
Tower Books
Unit 2/17 Rodborough Road
Frenchs Forest NSW 2086
Tel.: +61.2.9975.5566
Fax: +61.2.9975.5599
Email: towerbks@zip.com.au

STICKER NATION

THE BIG BOOK OF SUBVERSIVE STICKERS VOLUME 1

CREATED BY

SRINI KUMAR

Thank you to everyone who has supported our project so far!

AAAAAAAAAAAAA!!!!
Sometimes words get in the way. Imagine a crowd in protest holding up signs that just said "AAAAAA!" I'd like to see that.

ABANDON ANGER
What good does anger do you? When you do something in anger you're going to make others angry at you.

ABOLISH SWEATSHOPS
Millions of workers face a life of labor that doesn't provide for their needs. They deserve a fair wage and decent conditions.

ACCELERATE THE POSITIVE
Some memes are therapeutic and help the people who incorporate them live better lives. These must outpace toxic ones.

ADULTS ARE CONFUSED
Age doesn't necessarily confer wisdom. The world tends to get more complicated as we get older.

ADVERTISING IS POLLUTION
The swirl of madness disgorged by productopia affects the quality of our information intake and invades our space.

ALLERGIC TO BOREDOM
Boredom is activity that yields poor return on attention. Systems that stipulate boredom ought to be rendered obsolete.

ALL YOUR BASE ARE BELONG TO US
The Internet is capable of spreading *strange* messages. This one comes from a badly-translated Japanese video game.
http://www.allyourbasearebelongtous.com

All Your Fears Are Lies
The second we click into a "fear" mode, we become highly suggestible. We act without thinking and often make it worse.

ALTER THE STATE
Government seems to be here to stay. Unfortunately many who could improve it have no way to get their ideas across.

ANARCHY IS INEVITABLE
Entropy increases in any system. Why should the geopolitical system be any different?

ANGST IS LAME
There are a million reasons for any of us to be dissatisfied. It is therefore a poor choice to wallow in this dissatisfaction.

ANNOY THE BORING
My universe is divided into interesting and boring, rather than "good" and "evil."

ANTI-FASHION
People wear unique fashions to "make a statement." This substitution can only mean they have nothing at all to say.

ART NOT APATHY
Add more art into your life. Rather than withdrawing from life why not develop new ways to shape it?

ASK ME ABOUT MY LOW WAGES
Low wages are evidence that the social contract is a sham. We are engaged as robots in repetition unto obsolescence.

ASK QUESTIONS FREQUENTLY
The power to ask the questions in society is monopolized by those who have "all the answers."

ASSUME THIS PHONE IS TAPPED
Current technology bristles with potential for the violation of privacy, and it's improving all the time.

AVOID THE STUPID
We take on the qualities of the people who surround us. To get smarter, find a smarter environment for your mind.

BAD SEX SUCKS
Practice makes perfect! *[check out the Disinformation book EVERYTHING YOU KNOW ABOUT SEX IS WRONG! —ed.]*

BE PREPARED
Sort the options competing for your attention and connect rapidly with the resources that matter the most to you.

BECOME THE DOMINANT PARADIGM
A paradigm is an "approach," or a lens through which you perceive reality. A new way to see the world changes the world.

BEING HIP IS NOT ENOUGH
Modern kids have learned to make video and art fast and cheap. Imagine this talent channelled into work for change.

BEND SPACE-TIME
Picture the diffusion of your message into the mental environment surrounding it; the nature of the space itself may shift.

BE YOURSELF
It's not just what you "do" with your life, but who you are and where you're drawn as a result.

BLOCK THEOCRACY
"Theocracy means God is in control, and you are not."—*the Reverend Rod Parsley*   http://www.theocracywatch.org/

BORN TO CHILL
Don't let egos and external chaos chase your serenity away. Life is music; the rests are as important as the notes.

boy does high school ever suck
There is a difference between "education" and "learning." Why not teach young people subjects they really want to learn?

BUREAUCRACY RULES
The aim of the bureaucrat is CONTROL. The logic is that a controlled system is optimal. Human needs are merely friction.

CAN YOU ESCAPE?
Advertisers use repetitive, associative, and hypnotic subliminal suggestions to stimulate or reinforce various cravings.

CAPITALISM IS ORGANIZED CRIME
Every Board of Directors is a CONSPIRACY. Secrecy is the precondition of the typical corporate strategy of utter dominion.

CELEBRITY IS WORTHLESS
Attention is harvested by the media and celebrities drive the thresher. Zapped by cathode rays, many are scarred for life.

CENSORSHIP IS IMPOSSIBLE
The strategy of censorship makes perfect sense from the perspective of an authoritarian memeticist. They think it works.

CHALLENGE YOUR HABITS
We can be trained in behaviors imprinted upon us, or "get used to" behaviors that are bad for us in the long run.

CHANGE THE CHANNEL
Peer into adjacent parallel universes. There are aspects that are improvements upon ours. Import them into this one.

Strong ideas can alter the public's point of view despite deeply entrenched and culturally-endorsed opposing beliefs.

Complex systems emerge from complex individuals, natural chaos emerges. It takes balance to make good decisions.

When plans go astray it's usually because some foundation assumption has been made, skewing the whole process.

As children we demand a treat and receive it; as adults, perhaps we can learn to demand political reform as effectively.

We do not work to "produce," but so that we may eventually relax. We ought to structure our lives to get more freedom.

The toxic effects of smoking are causing a healthcare epidemic. Few products carry government warnings about cancer.

"The effects of [your] deeds actively create present and future experiences, thus making one responsible for one's own life." —*Wikipedia*
http://en.wikipedia.org/wiki/Karma

CHANGE YOUR MIND
CHAOTIC NEUTRAL
check your assumptions
children know everything
CHOOSE SLACK
CIGARETTES ARE AWFUL
CLEAR YOUR KARMA

Late-night bursts of caffeinated inspiration echo forever, winding like biorhythmic waves atwist the timelines of our lives.

There is no substitute for a genuine emotional connection with your goals to spur your drive to get your ideas across.

We have no control over our audience unless we control who's in it. Which is one reason this book is shrinkwrapped.

Moderation is going to spare you a lot of future headaches. When you get blitzed, you're taking chances!

A conspiracy of bureaucrats and plutocrats with a vision of technological utopia through surveillance has made big plans.

Corporations exist to maximize shareholder value. Their beer is brewed by some spreadsheet in Product Development.

The will of capital permeates democracy. The People have "special interests" unsupported by any lobby but ourselves.

COFFEE NOW DAMMIT
COMMUNICATE
CONFUSE EVERYONE
CONSIDER SOBRIETY
COPS ARE THE FUTURE
CORPORATE BEER SUCKS
corporations are government

Corporations were created to concentrate wealth. The truth can prove an inconvenient obstacle to boardroom schemes.

The click of recognition when people of similar outlook connect for the first time is the sound of society waking up.

If you generate information, people may be stimulated by your concepts and alter their behavior to fit your perspective.

Ancient Egyptians built pyramids in honor of their well-constructed hierarchical social system, which continues to this day.

Hypocrisy isn't just dishonesty; it's engaging in activities that runs counter to what you profess to believe.

I'm certain this sticker belongs somewhere in your social world.

The poison of cynicism is an anaesthetic. There are always alternatives and oblique strategies.

CORPORATIONS LIE
COULD YOU BE THE ONE?
CREATE YOUR OWN GODS
culture is engineered
CURB YOUR HYPOCRISY
CUTIE ON DUTY
CYNICS GO TO HELL

Don't pretend you're a loser just because it's "hip."

Belt out a harmonic counterpoint to the consolidated and barely opposed actions of the strong.

The easier you can predict a message, the less information that message contains. Shake up the infosphere with me!

Young kids are grouped into classes based on their supposed "intelligence" and we tend to stay in those roles forever.

This book is an attempt to make a difference in people's lives by highlighting the politics of *subliminal oppression*.

"And I think to myself.... what a wonderful world" —*Louis Armstrong*

Machines of war may be manned by humans, but the inhuman destruction they cause begs a pacifist response.

DARE TO BE SMART
DECLARE INDEPENDENCE
DEFEAT BOREDOM
DEFY ANALYSIS
DELUSIONS COMFY ENOUGH?
DISCOVER THE EARTH
DISTURB THE WAR

When most people profess belief, they expose deep confusion. We all relate to true freedom, but do you BELIEVE in it?

Even an infinitely advanced mathematical simulation model couldn't predict what you're about to create tomorrow.

Why do people ignore information that is very important to their own survival? Do they assume someone else will learn it?

Risk and reward are negatively correllated. Don't live a risky life, but you probably could use a few rewards now and then.

You can't always change your circumstances but you can instantly switch your role. The world needs your ideas!

You can create a new reality for yourself. You have the wisdom to apply this ability correctly. Trust yourself!

Labels stuck on our heads by the System are self-fulfilling prophecies. Reduced to labels we fit the spreadsheet nicely.

do you believe in liberation?
DO YOUR THING
DOES NOT EXIST
DON'T BE SUCH A WUSS
DON'T DELAY YOUR DREAM
DON'T GET CAUGHT
DON'T LABEL ME

DON'T LIE TO KIDS — Lying to kids will just teach them to lie to you. Develop an allergy to the taint of dishonesty and treat kids with respect.

DON'T POSTPONE JOY — Every moment has the potential for positive transfiguration. Maybe you're a little too busy for that hippy crap but it's the truth.

DON'T STOP BELIEVING — It takes strength to stay optimistic. Faith is free; you don't need a religion to access faith. Find something to believe in.

DON'T TREAD ON ME — The saga of American independence from the British crown has more secret history than can be easily summarized here.
http://www.disinfo.com/site/displayarticle12012.html

DRUGS MESS YOU UP — Each fragment of your physical and mental existence is staked out as potential paydirt by the pharmaceutical industry.

EAT MORE VEGGIES — Millions now living will never eat meat. Someday I'll write up my mom's recipes for South Indian food; y'all are missing out!

EDUCATE YOUR PARENTS — Many people cut their parents off right at the point in life where they're finally learning new information about the world.

ELECT YOURSELF — I'm sick of the echo chamber of modern democratic politics. I can see right through the dodges of politicians. You can too.

ELECTRONIC ANARCHIST — "Unity and self-expression fused in a force field of pulsating, undulating euphoria." —Simon Reynolds, _Generation Ecstasy_

END THE C.I.A. — "...the CIA continues to work with and protect those producing and shipping the drugs in the first place." —Preston Peet
http://www.disinfo.com/archive/pages/dossier/id182/pg1/

EQUALITY NOW! — I abhor the lie that diverse people are more DIFFERENT than SAME. Our individuality shouldn't slake our thirst for justice.

everybody is a star — I see constellations where others see dust. Innovation was once limited to serendipity, now it's a process involving YOU.

EVERYTHING IS COOL — Even the difficulties we face as a planet are _interesting_. View the static of society as an opportunity, not a threat.

EVERYTHING IS ENERGY — Give people stimulus as an _option_ to modify their environment, and you are making them richer. They'll return the favor.

EVOLUTION ISN'T OVER — When people get together, mutations emerge from the juxtaposition. Our minds evolve with new stimulus; why not our DNA?

express yourself — Each of us are forces of nature and it is as natural for us to seek expression as it is oxygen.

FASCISM IS SNEAKY — Assured by fiery slogans declaiming our liberty, we let culture, economy, church and state conspire against the real thing.

FAST FOOD IS FAT FOOD — "30,000 Americans die every year of obesity, more than the total annual toll of car accidents, firearms, drugs and alcohol combined."
http://www.disinfo.com/site/displayarticle6510.html

FEEL THE ONENESS — We emerge from the same gene pool. We belong to each other. Why do we let institutions and ugly ideology separate us?

FEMINISM FOREVER — Equal opportunity for men and women? Sounds great to me.

FIGHT FAT PHOBIA — We aren't "fat" or "not-fat"; we are bundles of energy and can change shape with the will of the moment.

FIGHT THE RIGHT — The demagogues of conservatism can claim popular support for their ideas because they're great at manipulating people.

FIND THE TIME TO READ — Sometimes I feel like the books are reading ME. Common literacy is a fairly modern development. Don't take it for granted!

FOLLOW YOUR HEART — "Hate your enemies/Save your friends/Find your place/Speak the truth."—Nirvana, "Radio Friendly Unit Shifter"

FORGE THE FUTURE — We can project our voice to vaccinate our friends from the toxic side effects of amoral hegemonic meme expansion.

FORGET YOUR FEARS — You see different things depending on your mood. If you approach life fearlessly different information can be unearthed...

FREE SPEECH ISN'T FREE — Technology has irreversibly granted us greater freedom of information dissemination. It isn't free, but at least it's cheaper.

FREEDOM OF INFORMATION — Explore the pathways and secrecy of information and ideas and how they reveal a very different view of our political world.

F@#% CENSORSHIP — This sticker is almost a paradox, but not quite.

FUN IS MY FUNCTION — There are many ways to contribute to a group, and making sure it's having fun is a critical role.

GANESHA LOVES YOU — Ganesha is the elephant-headed god in Hindu mythology. He just told me he's on your side.

GENERATE YOUR FATE — Develop a "script" that gets you what you want and deserve after you follow the plot. What are you going to achieve?

GET OVER IT — We have an incredible power to visualize our own futures. We can't afford negative thought-constructs in our minds.

GIMME NOISE — During the halcyon days of '80s metal I managed to get in to a few classic shows. My ears are still ringing.

GIVE ME ALL YOUR MONEY — You can PayPal me at srini@stickernation.com.

This is meant not as a description but as an imperative. The darkness vanishes when you light up your spirit.

Suburbia is a cultural quarantine. If you try to protect your kids by raising them in a bubble, someday it might burst.

These slogans are meant to stimulate your thought and action beyond just digging the phrase or the point of view.

Hierarchy and coercion are a drag. As your friends organize to achieve goals, consider alternative organizational models.

"...explosive technological growth... hide[s] neo-authoritarian mythic-membership structures used to control host populations." —Alex Burns
http://www.disinfo.com/archive/pages/dossier/id292/pg1/index.html

Expand your network by conveying your respect to a larger proportion of those you contact.

"Workin' all week, 9 to 5 for my money/So when the weekend comes I go get live with the honeys" —Tone-Loc, "Wild Thing"

Wander city streets and scan street signs for stickers and graffiti - a wavelength that transmits hectic cultural ferment.

Corruption makes a mockery of the clarion call of "free enterprise." Thieves and liars face not sanction but glory.

How do we learn foreign languages? Is it the rigid application of memory, or do we just catch the groove and roll with it?

Six strings, infinite possibilities. Teach kids how to use musical instruments instead of toy soldiers to reshape the world.

A system of language, syntax and symbolism is the basis for every distance interaction. Modern power is built on words.

Where does harmony come from? It's mathematical and magical; it involves physics and "psychics" in equal measure.

Hate is like friction and its sparks cause fires. What a waste, to spend one's time and energy hating other people.

Self-righteous punk rock pseudointelligentsia consumed their own scene with childish "sellout" labelling in the '90s.

My strategy is to provide my audience with tools to change minds. Is overconsumption a compulsion or a choice?

The history that's being made all around you is hard to analyze without some perspective. Wheels can spin both ways.

Find sources of spiritual nourishment where none had previously been thought to exist.

Your capacity to craft and transmit ideas is *power*. This power cannot remain a monopoly of mass media. It's yours.

The typical citizen does not grasp the reality of their situation because they refuse to listen to *that type* of information.

"The equal and inalienable rights of all are the foundation of freedom, justice and peace in the world" —the United Nations

How many cups of coffee have I had today? Eight? I have a job to do. No sleep 'til this is finished. I am unstoppable!

I chose the medium of stickers because each one is a "situation generator." The context of a sticker adds to its meaning.

I disown none of my life. I have made mistakes but I have learned a lot. The karma I generate is mine alone.

"The art of meta-communication lies in the art of concealing the art." —Alex Burns
http://www.disinfo.com/archive/pages/article/id705/pg1/

The words we use in conversation are just the ephemeral framework of quality interactions. They carry our *brain waves*.

It's inane to think that just because somebody shares some of your views they are a good person.

I wouldn't trade my spot in the universe with *anyone*. Would you?

"Good vs. evil" is much easier for consensus morality to implant in you. "Interesting vs. boring" is *always* your call.

The conceit of power is that only wealth and military action can change the circumstances of a nation. You and I can too.

Get me on stage with a bass and my surf rock battalion the Aquamen. Wild gyrations and mayhem triggered by rock'n'roll!

To what extent is the computer and its design a mirror of the way our own minds are configured? Can we "free the code"?

"We're not blocking traffic, we ARE traffic!" —Critical Mass rallying cry   http://critical-mass.info/howto/

"Woman is a ray of God; you could say that she is Creator, not created." —Rumi

You can create. You know you can. You've done it since you were a kid doodling instead of studying, and you'll never stop.

I STILL BELIEVE — I like open-ended statements like this one. I enjoy giving the user of my stickers room to define the words how they want.

I WANT JUSTICE — Few of the real violations against us are ever prosecuted. Justice is used as a harness to control segments of society.

IDEAS ARE FRACTAL — Ideas can be analyzed as if they are biological phenomena populating a "mental ecosystem" or sphere of human thought.

IDENTIFY YOUR OPTIONS — You exist as a nexus of reality and potential, and your potential is growing. Your options are worth a fortune.

IDEOLOGY IS IDIOTIC — Easy answers are tempting for starving minds. The common dialogue has to be too diverse to tolerate ideology.

I'M FEELING LUCKY — I'm thankful for all the lucky breaks I've received. It's easier to summon luck if you are capable of generating it from within.

I'M INNOCENT — It's smart to approach every day as if it were full of new things to discover. Let innocence spread among us.

i'm tired of being told what to think — I need to learn about the world, but the "news" filters information to present a consensus reality that's riddled with holes.

IMMORTALITY OR BUST — Led Zeppelin can't be replaced or competed against, like products can; they broadened our culture to accommodate them.

INFORMATION IS POWER — The design of our culture is engineered by human beings – why not you? Shape your ideas into a precision tool for change.

INCITE COOPERATION — There is so much to be done that can only be done with others. Frameworks for cooperation can be applied to any project.

JAZZ IS MY RELIGION — Without space for jazz, society was stifled. Jazz shifted the entire world culture towards flexibility, rhythm and soul.

JUST BE PURE — Unadulterated, no additives. Not from concentrate. You can apply your energy best when you refract it least.

JUST SAY OM — Feels good, doesn't it?

KEEP ABORTION LEGAL — Just how intrusive can the guardians of "morality" get? And how can "pro-life" citizens support torture, slavery and war?

KEEP DIGGING — I'm always surprised by the strange paths I take to arrive at new attitudes, information, ideas, tools and tactics.

KEEP YOUR EYES OPEN — Sort the options competing for your attention and connect rapidly with resources that matter the most to you.

KINDNESS IS STRENGTH — Everyone knows that true power is generosity, not mere riches. When you've got your act together why be a jerk?

KISS MORE HATE LESS — Maybe stickers can make the solution seem simpler than we all know it to be. Imagine if it were this easy. (Maybe it is!)

KNOW YOUR RIGHTS — The most effective way for your rights to be systematically violated is to suppress your knowledge that those rights even exist.

LAUGH AT POLITICIANS — We often find politics dull, irrelevant and dispensable. Why not kick back and enjoy the show?

LEARN TO COOK — Garbage in, garbage out. Control of your nutrition is critical if you want to put out positive energy. It's a lot cheaper too!

LET MY PEOPLE GO — We perceive space for a new harmony in the chant of human discourse, a new voice to alter the tempo of our civilization.

let the good times roll — Today is going to ROCK. This is the sticker that's on my guitar amp.

LET'S GET BUSY Y'ALL — I have no control over what you're going to get out of this book. All I can hope is that it helps you crank it up a notch.

LET'S INVADE SATURN NEXT — Why bother with earthbound imperialism when there are entire glorious planets we have yet to colonize?

LIBIDO ERGO SUM — "Every time I comb my hair/Thoughts of u get in my eyes/U're a sinner, I don't care/I just want your creamy thighs" —Prince, "Erotic City"

LIBRARIES ARE AWESOME — Language has evolved along with humankind, like the technology for its reproduction. Libraries are shrines of language.

LIFE IS BEAUTIFUL — Everybody alive has a mission; they just might not have run across it yet. Even adversaries add energy to your mix.

LIMIT YOUR CONSUMPTION — Our purchase patterns are locked in; firms value future consumption as a perpetuity as long as they fund their ad budget.

LINUX IS POWER — Free the source code and the users will refine the program. This is a powerful metaphor for my vision of political change.

LISTEN TO COLLEGE RADIO — Radio is run by an oligopoly of the insipid. College radio delivers secret sounds for those with ears to hear.

LISTEN TO MARSHALL MCLUHAN — There is a pattern that can be puzzled out from the hegemonic use of messaging to govern humankind.

LITTLE IS KNOWN — We look at the beliefs of the Middle Ages and marvel at their innocence and ignorance. What will the future say of us?

LIVE AND LET LIVE — Shrug off bitterness and forsake retribution. What you can scream at someone can also be written down.

ALL YOUR BASE ARE BELONG TO US

SAY IT WITH STICKERS * WWW.STICKERNATION.COM ©2006

All Your Fears Are Lies

SAY IT WITH STICKERS * WWW.STICKERNATION.COM ©2006

ALTER THE STATE

SAY IT WITH STICKERS * WWW.STICKERNATION.COM ©2006

ANARCHY IS INEVITABLE

SAY IT WITH STICKERS * WWW.STICKERNATION.COM ©2006

ANGST IS LAME

SAY IT WITH STICKERS * WWW.STICKERNATION.COM ©2006

ANNOY THE BORING

SAY IT WITH STICKERS * WWW.STICKERNATION.COM ©2006

ANTI-FASHION

SAY IT WITH STICKERS * WWW.STICKERNATION.COM ©2006

AAAAAAAAAAAAAAA!!!!

SAY IT WITH STICKERS * WWW.STICKERNATION.COM
©2006

ABANDON ANGER

SAY IT WITH STICKERS * WWW.STICKERNATION.COM
©2006

ABOLISH SWEATSHOPS

SAY IT WITH STICKERS * WWW.STICKERNATION.COM
©2006

ACCELERATE THE POSITIVE

SAY IT WITH STICKERS * WWW.STICKERNATION.COM
©2006

ADULTS ARE CONFUSED

SAY IT WITH STICKERS * WWW.STICKERNATION.COM
©2006

ADVERTISING IS POLLUTION

SAY IT WITH STICKERS * WWW.STICKERNATION.COM
©2006

ALLERGIC TO BOREDOM

SAY IT WITH STICKERS * WWW.STICKERNATION.COM
©2006

ART NOT APATHY

SAY IT WITH STICKERS * WWW.STICKERNATION.COM ©2006

ASK ME ABOUT MY LOW WAGES

SAY IT WITH STICKERS * WWW.STICKERNATION.COM ©2006

ASK QUESTIONS FREQUENTLY

SAY IT WITH STICKERS * WWW.STICKERNATION.COM ©2006

ASSUME THIS PHONE IS TAPPED

SAY IT WITH STICKERS * WWW.STICKERNATION.COM ©2006

AVOID THE STUPID

SAY IT WITH STICKERS * WWW.STICKERNATION.COM ©2006

BAD SEX SUCKS

SAY IT WITH STICKERS * WWW.STICKERNATION.COM ©2006

BE PREPARED

BECOME THE DOMINANT PARADIGM

SAY IT WITH STICKERS * WWW.STICKERNATION.COM

BEING HIP IS NOT ENOUGH

SAY IT WITH STICKERS * WWW.STICKERNATION.COM

BEND SPACE-TIME

SAY IT WITH STICKERS * WWW.STICKERNATION.COM

BE YOURSELF

SAY IT WITH STICKERS * WWW.STICKERNATION.COM

BLOCK THEOCRACY

SAY IT WITH STICKERS * WWW.STICKERNATION.COM

BORN TO CHILL

SAY IT WITH STICKERS * WWW.STICKERNATION.COM

boy does high school ever suck

BUREAUCRACY RULES

SAY IT WITH STICKERS * WWW.STICKERNATION.CO

CAN YOU ESCAPE?

SAY IT WITH STICKERS * WWW.STICKERNATION.CO

CAPITALISM IS ORGANIZED CRIME

SAY IT WITH STICKERS * WWW.STICKERNATION.CO

CELEBRITY IS WORTHLESS

SAY IT WITH STICKERS * WWW.STICKERNATION.CO

CENSORSHIP IS IMPOSSIBLE

SAY IT WITH STICKERS * WWW.STICKERNATION.COM

CHALLENGE YOUR HABITS

SAY IT WITH STICKERS * WWW.STICKERNATION.COM

CHANGE THE CHANNEL

SAY IT WITH STICKERS * WWW.STICKERNATION.CO

CHANGE YOUR MIND

SAY IT WITH STICKERS * WWW.STICKERNATION.COM ©2006

CHAOTIC NEUTRAL

SAY IT WITH STICKERS * WWW.STICKERNATION.COM ©2006

check your assumptions

SAY IT WITH STICKERS * WWW.STICKERNATION.COM ©2006

children know everything

SAY IT WITH STICKERS * WWW.STICKERNATION.COM ©2006

CHOOSE SLACK

SAY IT WITH STICKERS * WWW.STICKERNATION.COM ©2006

CIGARETTES ARE AWFUL

SAY IT WITH STICKERS * WWW.STICKERNATION.COM ©2006

CLEAR YOUR KARMA

SAY IT WITH STICKERS * WWW.STICKERNATION.COM ©2006

COFFEE NOW DAMMIT

SAY IT WITH STICKERS * WWW.STICKERNATION.COM ©2006

COMMUNICATE

SAY IT WITH STICKERS * WWW.STICKERNATION.COM ©2006

CONSIDER SOBRIETY

SAY IT WITH STICKERS * WWW.STICKERNATION.COM ©2006

COPS ARE THE FUTURE

SAY IT WITH STICKERS * WWW.STICKERNATION.COM ©2006

CORPORATE BEER SUCKS

SAY IT WITH STICKERS * WWW.STICKERNATION.COM ©2006

corporations are government

SAY IT WITH STICKERS * WWW.STICKERNATION.COM

CORPORATIONS LIE
SAY IT WITH STICKERS * WWW.STICKERNATION.COM ©2006

COULD YOU BE THE ONE?
SAY IT WITH STICKERS * WWW.STICKERNATION.COM ©2006

CREATE YOUR OWN GODS
SAY IT WITH STICKERS * WWW.STICKERNATION.COM ©2006

culture is engineered
SAY IT WITH STICKERS * WWW.STICKERNATION.COM ©2006

CURB YOUR HYPOCRISY
SAY IT WITH STICKERS * WWW.STICKERNATION.COM ©2006

CUTIE ON DUTY
SAY IT WITH STICKERS * WWW.STICKERNATION.COM ©2006

CYNICS GO TO HELL
SAY IT WITH STICKERS * WWW.STICKERNATION.COM ©2006

DARE TO BE SMART

SAY IT WITH STICKERS * WWW.STICKERNATION.COM ©2006

DECLARE INDEPENDENCE

SAY IT WITH STICKERS * WWW.STICKERNATION.COM ©2006

DEFEAT BOREDOM

SAY IT WITH STICKERS * WWW.STICKERNATION.COM ©2006

DEFY ANALYSIS

SAY IT WITH STICKERS * WWW.STICKERNATION.COM ©2006

DELUSIONS COMFY ENOUGH?

SAY IT WITH STICKERS * WWW.STICKERNATION.COM ©2006

DISCOVER THE EARTH

SAY IT WITH STICKERS * WWW.STICKERNATION.COM ©2006

DISTURB THE WAR

SAY IT WITH STICKERS * WWW.STICKERNATION.COM

do you believe in liberation?

SAY IT WITH STICKERS * WWW.STICKERNATION.COM
©2006

DO YOUR THING

SAY IT WITH STICKERS * WWW.STICKERNATION.COM
©2006

DOES NOT EXIST

SAY IT WITH STICKERS * WWW.STICKERNATION.COM
©2006

DON'T BE SUCH A WUSS

SAY IT WITH STICKERS * WWW.STICKERNATION.COM
©2006

DON'T DELAY YOUR DREAM

SAY IT WITH STICKERS * WWW.STICKERNATION.COM
©2006

DON'T GET CAUGHT

SAY IT WITH STICKERS * WWW.STICKERNATION.COM
©2006

DON'T LABEL ME

SAY IT WITH STICKERS * WWW.STICKERNATION.COM

DON'T LIE TO KIDS

SAY IT WITH STICKERS * WWW.STICKERNATION.COM
©2006

DON'T POSTPONE JOY

SAY IT WITH STICKERS * WWW.STICKERNATION.COM
©2006

DON'T STOP BELIEVING

SAY IT WITH STICKERS * WWW.STICKERNATION.COM
©2006

DON'T TREAD ON ME

SAY IT WITH STICKERS * WWW.STICKERNATION.COM
©2006

DRUGS MESS YOU UP

SAY IT WITH STICKERS * WWW.STICKERNATION.COM
©2006

EAT MORE VEGGIES

SAY IT WITH STICKERS * WWW.STICKERNATION.COM
©2006

EDUCATE YOUR PARENTS

SAY IT WITH STICKERS * WWW.STICKERNATION.COM

ELECT YOURSELF

SAY IT WITH STICKERS * WWW.STICKERNATION.COM ©2006

ELECTRONIC ANARCHIST

SAY IT WITH STICKERS * WWW.STICKERNATION.COM ©2006

END THE C.I.A.

SAY IT WITH STICKERS * WWW.STICKERNATION.COM ©2006

EQUALITY NOW!

SAY IT WITH STICKERS * WWW.STICKERNATION.COM ©2006

everybody is a star

SAY IT WITH STICKERS * WWW.STICKERNATION.COM ©2006

EVERYTHING IS COOL

SAY IT WITH STICKERS * WWW.STICKERNATION.COM ©2006

EVERYTHING IS ENERGY

SAY IT WITH STICKERS * WWW.STICKERNATION.COM

EVOLUTION ISN'T OVER

SAY IT WITH STICKERS * WWW.STICKERNATION.COM ©2006

express yourself

SAY IT WITH STICKERS * WWW.STICKERNATION.COM ©2006

FASCISM IS SNEAKY

SAY IT WITH STICKERS * WWW.STICKERNATION.COM ©2006

FAST FOOD IS FAT FOOD

SAY IT WITH STICKERS * WWW.STICKERNATION.COM ©2006

FEEL THE ONENESS

SAY IT WITH STICKERS * WWW.STICKERNATION.COM ©2006

FEMINISM FOREVER

SAY IT WITH STICKERS * WWW.STICKERNATION.COM ©2006

FIGHT FAT PHOBIA

SAY IT WITH STICKERS * WWW.STICKERNATION.COM ©2006

FIGHT THE RIGHT

SAY IT WITH STICKERS * WWW.STICKERNATION.COM
©2006

FIND THE TIME TO READ

SAY IT WITH STICKERS * WWW.STICKERNATION.COM
©2006

FOLLOW YOUR HEART

SAY IT WITH STICKERS * WWW.STICKERNATION.COM
©2006

FORGE THE FUTURE

SAY IT WITH STICKERS * WWW.STICKERNATION.COM
©2006

FORGET YOUR FEARS

SAY IT WITH STICKERS * WWW.STICKERNATION.COM
©2006

FREE SPEECH ISN'T FREE

SAY IT WITH STICKERS * WWW.STICKERNATION.COM
©2006

FREEDOM OF INFORMATION

SAY IT WITH STICKERS * WWW.STICKERNATION.COM

F@#% CENSORSHIP

SAY IT WITH STICKERS * WWW.STICKERNATION.COM ©2006

FUN IS MY FUNCTION

SAY IT WITH STICKERS * WWW.STICKERNATION.COM ©2006

GANESHA LOVES YOU

SAY IT WITH STICKERS * WWW.STICKERNATION.COM ©2006

GENERATE YOUR FATE

SAY IT WITH STICKERS * WWW.STICKERNATION.COM ©2006

GET OVER IT

SAY IT WITH STICKERS * WWW.STICKERNATION.COM ©2006

GIMME NOISE

SAY IT WITH STICKERS * WWW.STICKERNATION.COM ©2006

GIVE ME ALL YOUR MONEY

SAY IT WITH STICKERS * WWW.STICKERNATION.COM

GLOW IN THE DARK

SAY IT WITH STICKERS * WWW.STICKERNATION.COM
©2006

GO BACK TO YOUR SUBURB

SAY IT WITH STICKERS * WWW.STICKERNATION.COM
©2006

GO BEYOND SLOGANS

SAY IT WITH STICKERS * WWW.STICKERNATION.COM
©2006

GO TRIBAL

SAY IT WITH STICKERS * WWW.STICKERNATION.COM
©2006

God is big business.

SAY IT WITH STICKERS * WWW.STICKERNATION.COM
©2006

GOD IS OTHER PEOPLE

SAY IT WITH STICKERS * WWW.STICKERNATION.COM
©2006

GOTTA LOVE HOTTIES

SAY IT WITH STICKERS * WWW.STICKERNATION.COM
©2006

SET ME FREE

SAY IT WITH STICKERS * WWW.STICKERNATION.COM ©2006

SEX TOYS ROCK

SAY IT WITH STICKERS * WWW.STICKERNATION.COM ©2006

SHHHHHHH. LISTEN.

SAY IT WITH STICKERS * WWW.STICKERNATION.COM ©2006

SMASH PATRIARCHY

SAY IT WITH STICKERS * WWW.STICKERNATION.COM ©2006

SOCIETY IS SPASTIC

SAY IT WITH STICKERS * WWW.STICKERNATION.COM ©2006

SPARE THE AIR

SAY IT WITH STICKERS * WWW.STICKERNATION.COM ©2006

SPIN WON'T HIDE A LIE

SAY IT WITH STICKERS * WWW.STICKERNATION.COM

STAMP OUT HUNGER

SAY IT WITH STICKERS * WWW.STICKERNATION.COM
©2006

STOP FAKING IT

SAY IT WITH STICKERS * WWW.STICKERNATION.COM
©2006

STOP LIVING LIKE VEAL

SAY IT WITH STICKERS * WWW.STICKERNATION.COM
©2006

STUDENT POWER

SAY IT WITH STICKERS * WWW.STICKERNATION.COM
©2006

SUPPORT SUSTAINABLE SYSTEMS

SAY IT WITH STICKERS * WWW.STICKERNATION.COM
©2006

take nothing for granted

SAY IT WITH STICKERS * WWW.STICKERNATION.COM
©2006

TALK NERDY TO ME

SAY IT WITH STICKERS * WWW.STICKERNATION.COM

TAO IS ETERNAL
SAY IT WITH STICKERS * WWW.STICKERNATION.COM ©2006

TAX THE RICH
SAY IT WITH STICKERS * WWW.STICKERNATION.COM ©2006

TEAR GAS SUCKS
SAY IT WITH STICKERS * WWW.STICKERNATION.COM ©2006

TELEVISION IS SEXIST
SAY IT WITH STICKERS * WWW.STICKERNATION.COM ©2006

TERMINATE PREJUDICE
SAY IT WITH STICKERS * WWW.STICKERNATION.COM ©2006

THANK GOD I'M AGNOSTIC
SAY IT WITH STICKERS * WWW.STICKERNATION.COM ©2006

thank you for not screwing me over
SAY IT WITH STICKERS * WWW.STICKERNATION.COM ©2006

The Best Is Yet To Come

SAY IT WITH STICKERS * WWW.STICKERNATION.COM

the ends justify the memes

SAY IT WITH STICKERS * WWW.STICKERNATION.COM

the geeks shall inherit the earth

SAY IT WITH STICKERS * WWW.STICKERNATION.COM

THE ICE CAPS ARE MELTING

SAY IT WITH STICKERS * WWW.STICKERNATION.COM

THE INTERNET CHANGED MY LIFE

SAY IT WITH STICKERS * WWW.STICKERNATION.COM

THE ONLY CONSTANT IS CHANGE

SAY IT WITH STICKERS * WWW.STICKERNATION.COM

THE STREETS ARE ALIVE

SAY IT WITH STICKERS * WWW.STICKERNATION.COM

GRAFFITI MAKES SENSE

SAY IT WITH STICKERS * WWW.STICKERNATION.COM ©2006

GREED IS BAD

SAY IT WITH STICKERS * WWW.STICKERNATION.COM ©2006

GROOVE IS LIFE

SAY IT WITH STICKERS * WWW.STICKERNATION.COM ©2006

GUITARS NOT BOMBS

SAY IT WITH STICKERS * WWW.STICKERNATION.COM ©2006

HACK THE PROGRAM

SAY IT WITH STICKERS * WWW.STICKERNATION.COM ©2006

HARMONY HEALS

SAY IT WITH STICKERS * WWW.STICKERNATION.COM ©2006

HATE IS FOR WUSSES

SAY IT WITH STICKERS * WWW.STICKERNATION.COM

HAVE I SOLD OUT?

SAY IT WITH STICKERS * WWW.STICKERNATION.COM ©2006

HEAL THE PLANET

SAY IT WITH STICKERS * WWW.STICKERNATION.COM ©2006

HISTORY IS A LOOP

SAY IT WITH STICKERS * WWW.STICKERNATION.COM ©2006

HOPE SPRINGS ETERNAL

SAY IT WITH STICKERS * WWW.STICKERNATION.COM ©2006

HOW DEEP IS YOUR POWER?

SAY IT WITH STICKERS * WWW.STICKERNATION.COM ©2006

HOW DO YOU KNOW?

SAY IT WITH STICKERS * WWW.STICKERNATION.COM ©2006

HUMAN RIGHTS

SAY IT WITH STICKERS * WWW.STICKERNATION.COM

HYPERACTIVIST

SAY IT WITH STICKERS * WWW.STICKERNATION.COM
©2006

I AM A SITUATIONIST

SAY IT WITH STICKERS * WWW.STICKERNATION.COM
©2006

I AM RESPONSIBLE

SAY IT WITH STICKERS * WWW.STICKERNATION.COM
©2006

i am the best artist

SAY IT WITH STICKERS * WWW.STICKERNATION.COM
©2006

I CAN READ YOUR MIND

SAY IT WITH STICKERS * WWW.STICKERNATION.COM
©2006

I CAN'T BE YOU

SAY IT WITH STICKERS * WWW.STICKERNATION.COM
©2006

I BELIEVE IN ME

SAY IT WITH STICKERS * WWW.STICKERNATION.COM

I find myself fascinating.

SAY IT WITH STICKERS * WWW.STICKERNATION.COM ©2006

I JUST CHANGED THE WORLD

SAY IT WITH STICKERS * WWW.STICKERNATION.COM ©2006

I ♥ ROCKING OUT

SAY IT WITH STICKERS * WWW.STICKERNATION.COM ©2006

I ♥ SOURCE CODE

SAY IT WITH STICKERS * WWW.STICKERNATION.COM ©2006

I LOVE THIS BIKE

SAY IT WITH STICKERS * WWW.STICKERNATION.COM ©2006

I LOVE WOMEN

SAY IT WITH STICKERS * WWW.STICKERNATION.COM ©2006

I LOVE YOU

SAY IT WITH STICKERS * WWW.STICKERNATION.COM

I STILL BELIEVE
SAY IT WITH STICKERS * WWW.STICKERNATION.COM
©2006

I WANT JUSTICE
SAY IT WITH STICKERS * WWW.STICKERNATION.COM
©2006

IDEAS ARE FRACTAL
SAY IT WITH STICKERS * WWW.STICKERNATION.COM
©2006

IDENTIFY YOUR OPTIONS
SAY IT WITH STICKERS * WWW.STICKERNATION.COM
©2006

IDEOLOGY IS IDIOTIC
SAY IT WITH STICKERS * WWW.STICKERNATION.COM
©2006

I'M FEELING LUCKY
SAY IT WITH STICKERS * WWW.STICKERNATION.COM
©2006

I'M INNOCENT
SAY IT WITH STICKERS * WWW.STICKERNATION.COM

i'm tired of being told what to think

SAY IT WITH STICKERS * WWW.STICKERNATION.COM
©2006

IMMORTALITY OR BUST

SAY IT WITH STICKERS * WWW.STICKERNATION.COM
©2006

INFORMATION IS POWER

SAY IT WITH STICKERS * WWW.STICKERNATION.COM
©2006

INCITE COOPERATION

SAY IT WITH STICKERS * WWW.STICKERNATION.COM
©2006

JAZZ IS MY RELIGION

SAY IT WITH STICKERS * WWW.STICKERNATION.COM
©2006

JUST BE PURE

SAY IT WITH STICKERS * WWW.STICKERNATION.COM
©2006

JUST SAY OM

SAY IT WITH STICKERS * WWW.STICKERNATION.COM

KEEP ABORTION LEGAL

SAY IT WITH STICKERS * WWW.STICKERNATION.CO

KEEP DIGGING

SAY IT WITH STICKERS * WWW.STICKERNATION.CO

KEEP YOUR EYES OPEN

SAY IT WITH STICKERS * WWW.STICKERNATION.CO

KINDNESS IS STRENGTH

SAY IT WITH STICKERS * WWW.STICKERNATION.CO

KISS MORE HATE LESS

SAY IT WITH STICKERS * WWW.STICKERNATION.CO

KNOW YOUR RIGHTS

SAY IT WITH STICKERS * WWW.STICKERNATION.CO

LAUGH AT POLITICIANS

SAY IT WITH STICKERS * WWW.STICKERNATION.CO

LEARN TO COOK
SAY IT WITH STICKERS * WWW.STICKERNATION.COM ©2006

LET MY PEOPLE GO
SAY IT WITH STICKERS * WWW.STICKERNATION.COM ©2006

let the good times roll
SAY IT WITH STICKERS * WWW.STICKERNATION.COM ©2006

LET'S GET BUSY Y'ALL
SAY IT WITH STICKERS * WWW.STICKERNATION.COM ©2006

LET'S INVADE SATURN NEXT
SAY IT WITH STICKERS * WWW.STICKERNATION.COM ©2006

LIBIDO ERGO SUM
SAY IT WITH STICKERS * WWW.STICKERNATION.COM ©2006

LIBRARIES ARE AWESOME
SAY IT WITH STICKERS * WWW.STICKERNATION.COM

LIFE IS BEAUTIFUL

SAY IT WITH STICKERS * WWW.STICKERNATION.COM
©2006

LIMIT YOUR CONSUMPTION

SAY IT WITH STICKERS * WWW.STICKERNATION.COM
©2006

LINUX IS POWER

SAY IT WITH STICKERS * WWW.STICKERNATION.COM
©2006

LISTEN TO COLLEGE RADIO

SAY IT WITH STICKERS * WWW.STICKERNATION.COM
©2006

LISTEN TO MARSHALL MCLUHAN

SAY IT WITH STICKERS * WWW.STICKERNATION.COM
©2006

LITTLE IS KNOWN

SAY IT WITH STICKERS * WWW.STICKERNATION.COM
©2006

LIVE AND LET LIVE

SAY IT WITH STICKERS * WWW.STICKERNATION.COM

LIVE IT UP

SAY IT WITH STICKERS * WWW.STICKERNATION.CO ©200

LIVE LONG AND PROSPER

SAY IT WITH STICKERS * WWW.STICKERNATION.CO ©200

LIVE THE CHAOS

SAY IT WITH STICKERS * WWW.STICKERNATION.CO ©200

LOGIC IS YOUR FRIEND

SAY IT WITH STICKERS * WWW.STICKERNATION.CO ©200

LOOK ALIVE

SAY IT WITH STICKERS * WWW.STICKERNATION.CO ©200

LOST IN SPACE

SAY IT WITH STICKERS * WWW.STICKERNATION.CO ©20

LOUDER THAN THE MEDIA

SAY IT WITH STICKERS * WWW.STICKERNATION.CO

LOVE IS THE ANSWER

SAY IT WITH STICKERS * WWW.STICKERNATION.COM
©2006

MAKE IT STOP

SAY IT WITH STICKERS * WWW.STICKERNATION.COM
©2006

MAKE LOVE NOT WORK

SAY IT WITH STICKERS * WWW.STICKERNATION.COM
©2006

MAKE YUPPIES REPENT

SAY IT WITH STICKERS * WWW.STICKERNATION.COM
©2006

MASS MEDIA MAKES MORONS

SAY IT WITH STICKERS * WWW.STICKERNATION.COM
©2006

MAYBE PARTYING WILL HELP

SAY IT WITH STICKERS * WWW.STICKERNATION.COM
©2006

MEET US IN ORBIT

SAY IT WITH STICKERS * WWW.STICKERNATION.COM

MELT ALL GUNS

SAY IT WITH STICKERS * WWW.STICKERNATION.COM ©2006

MONEY ISN'T WEALTH

SAY IT WITH STICKERS * WWW.STICKERNATION.COM ©2006

Money Is Not Our God

SAY IT WITH STICKERS * WWW.STICKERNATION.COM ©2006

MORE ORGASMS FEWER KIDS

SAY IT WITH STICKERS * WWW.STICKERNATION.COM ©2006

MORE POINTLESS LAWS

SAY IT WITH STICKERS * WWW.STICKERNATION.COM ©2006

MOSH CLOCKWISE

SAY IT WITH STICKERS * WWW.STICKERNATION.COM ©2006

MP3 IS NOT A CRIME

SAY IT WITH STICKERS * WWW.STICKERNATION.COM

music keeps me sane

SAY IT WITH STICKERS * WWW.STICKERNATION.COM ©2006

MY BRAIN HURTS

SAY IT WITH STICKERS * WWW.STICKERNATION.COM ©2006

MY GOVERNMENT IS NUTS

SAY IT WITH STICKERS * WWW.STICKERNATION.COM ©2006

MY TECHNOLOGY RULES

SAY IT WITH STICKERS * WWW.STICKERNATION.COM ©2006

MY WORD IS MY BOND

SAY IT WITH STICKERS * WWW.STICKERNATION.COM ©2006

NATURE IS PISSED

SAY IT WITH STICKERS * WWW.STICKERNATION.COM ©2006

NAZIS ARE PATHETIC

SAY IT WITH STICKERS * WWW.STICKERNATION.COM

NEVER GIVE UP

SAY IT WITH STICKERS * WWW.STICKERNATION.COM
©2006

NO ROOM FOR PHONIES

SAY IT WITH STICKERS * WWW.STICKERNATION.COM
©2006

NO WORRIES

SAY IT WITH STICKERS * WWW.STICKERNATION.COM
©2006

NOBODY HATES YOU

SAY IT WITH STICKERS * WWW.STICKERNATION.COM
©2006

ONE THING LEADS TO ANOTHER

SAY IT WITH STICKERS * WWW.STICKERNATION.COM
©2006

ONLY GOD CAN JUDGE ME

SAY IT WITH STICKERS * WWW.STICKERNATION.COM
©2006

ooh! ooh! can I be a DJ too? please?

SAY IT WITH STICKERS * WWW.STICKERNATION.COM

**Talking up stickers at Webzine2005
(http://www.webzine2005.com).**

context.

Words are all around us, but we hardly ever think about them. The ideas we might remember, but the actual words we usually forget unless they find some kind of premium positioning in our minds. We study books and the actual words whip away in the wind, leaving only the general idea remaining. We can overcome this ignorance of words by adopting a strategy of memorization; there are people who have *pi* memorized to thousands of digits, and others who spend their weekends reciting Shakespeare. But for most of us this route is impractical. Our memory is adapted to remember information that is specifically designed to be remembered. Writing and imagery are creative processes, but there are formats and styles that are adapted to the way our memory works.

History reports many instances where a sharp little idea has carved out a new course for the river of consensus reality. All language is a realignment of consciousness. When we speak in any given moment we do so in order to participate in it. A message is generated in our mind, articulated by our voice, heard by another's ear; everything changes. Your speech shifts the attention — and thereby the "known universe" — of those within earshot.

We swim in a sea of information. A system of language, syntax and symbolism is the foundation of every interaction we have with our friends or with corporations. The latter form of social interaction — advertising and marketing — is augmented by big money. There is a limited supply of human attention but the market demands more and more of it and will resort to almost anything to get and keep it. Wouldn't it be great if we could spread grassroots ideas as effectively?

Our attention spans have been studied very carefully. The advertising industry in the post-World War II era, as related by Vance Packard in his 1957 book *The Hidden Persuaders*, conducted a thorough analysis of the way we think about products which continues today. Some of this research led to the application of basic psychological tactics once used by despotic regimes, such as repetitive, associative, and hypnotic subliminal suggestions to stimulate or reinforce various cravings. The predictability of our purchase patterns is so airtight that most firms bet that future consumption is "locked in" as long as they advertise. The elite is in effect!

Politicians poll us to determine what to say on the stump; their managers fret about shaping target minds into voting blocs and action campaigns. Corporations run focus groups to tell *them* how to tell *us* what to do. Thinktanks weave cushions of words to soften their client politicians' harsh policies. Strategists develop plans for responses to our natural resistance to their domination.

Stickers cut through the attention clutter of modern society. Stickers transform household objects into advocates for your idea. Turn a bike into a megaphone against imperialism or vice; make your refrigerator a source of positive affirmation. Stickers break the monopoly that mass media pretends it still holds. Stickers are a form of ventriloquism: things can *speak*. The concept of *broadcast stickering* — not just having one for yourself but giving them out to your friends — is what StickerNation is all about.

Ideas are affected by the manner in which they're expressed. Each of the stickers in this book is a

HERMENEUTICS

explains what we can learn from what we read. how can you really delve into the works you encounter? where can you apply what you learn? how can you get a feel for how the authors lived their lives and formed their attitudes? what was the world LIKE when a piece was written? how can you judge the ideas you come across in it and fit them into a useful framework? for centuries philosophers studied what we can decipher and learn from ancient and modern works. hermeneutics is the analysis of real-world effects on readers by **the strength of ideas alone.**

hermeneutics also studies television, radio, film, theater, politics and other forms of deliberate information transfer. for instance, I develop messages for stickers by considering how well they will transfer my attitudes to my audience and whether they're likely to act on the suggestions I offer if they're equipped to act on what they learn. if I scream until I'm hoarse what's the point; if I hear echoes out there in the social landscape, however, perhaps the echoes will resonate until true freedom is uniformly distributed throughout the world. **together the People can muster a sustained roar.**

what does the text actually say? what's the voice used to convey the message? why is that voice chosen? what motivated the writer? what words are used? what is the logic behind their choice?

literal

you might find the voices of different writers to have an effect on what you get out of the text; grammar and emphasis can lead you towards or away from conclusions.

The reason I make stickers is because when I sit down to write, I want to affect the world. I don't know what's best for anyone other than me, but it sure took me long enough to figure

EVERY TEXT
INTERPRET

the relationship between a person and the book they're reading is absolutely dependent on that person's character: their social situation their experience and their ability to alter their environment, ideas they harbor, and their behavior.

moral

what does it mean to the READER? does the text present an archetype? how is it going to affect the reader's life? what's the reader supposed to get out of it? how is it going to affect the lives of its various readers?

what does the text EVOKE?
what does it RESEMBLE?
what feelings do you get when
you read it? does it tie in with
something else you've felt or
experienced? does it give you
clues to handle situations?

allegorical

there is often a
"hermetic seal" around
the real wisdom
contained in art or text.
**you need to carefully
scrutinize a creation
to get at its truths.**
what you learn depends
on where YOU are in life
and when you return to
a work you often learn
something new. history
presents us a vast array
of voices. why did they
put forth their efforts?
what are they trying to
tell us? what emotional
interpretations might
varying audiences make
of a given work? why?
hermeneutics asks:
**how will others see
THIS set of words?**

when you translate
the symbols you
interact with the text.
you might have to dig
deep to get at the
true meaning of a text
and draw parallels
between the text and
other works or
experiences you've
faced in real life.

**out what little I do
know and I thought
I'd share some of
it. Why do I make
stickers? Let's discuss
a key element of the
logic I follow when I
create stickers:
HERMENEUTICS.**

HAS FOUR
ATIONS...

is the text honest? is
it interesting to you,
or is it indicative of
the existence of a
group of humans with
beliefs or interests
that contrast with
yours? is it going to
change anything?

**every work of art or
text has wisdom
encoded in it.** it might
be wisdom you don't
need or like but the text
itself is there to reflect
events and ideas
relevant to the world as
it was seen from the
creator's eyes. the
wisdom can be directly
stated or inferred by
readers. various media
have different features
and benefits regarding
information transfer. I
wanted people to find
ways to work my words
into their surroundings,
**so I chose stickers to
get my ideas across.**
StickerNation lets you
make stickers too.

metaphysical

how does this text help us
understand the deeper
meaning of life and the
universe? what is going to be
the historical impact of this
text? what groups will it
affect? will it be read again?

gateway — to adjacent ideas, to other people and their rock and roll bands, to oblique issues that the popular media has ignored.

I started StickerNation.com in 2001 to help people get from "I've got an idea!" to a stack of stickers as fast as possible. If you print your idea up on stickers you can watch it "spread." Stickers help people remember; they keep repeating your message until they're worn out or torn down. The result can be a slow diffusion of the message into the mental environment surrounding it; the shape and nature of the space may change. A "meme" is a word that's starting to circulate on the internet in academia that has made me think a lot about the nature of ideas and how they spread. A meme is a "contagious" idea that seems to pass between people through adoption and mimicry. The term was created as a metaphor to relate the evolution of ideas to genetic evolution. StickerNation.com is a *meme factory.*

Memes are analogous to "genes"; through the concept of memes and their associated study, "memetics," ideas can be analyzed as if they were biological phenomena. Genes guide the development of species as they evolve; memes form the framework of the collective dialogue. Memes reproduce through communication networks and face-to-face contact between people. Like genes, they often program the characteristics and behavior of their hosts. Memes are made by advertising agencies and songwriters and reproduced by photocopiers and radio stations. Certain memes, like the behavior of cigarette smoking, can be toxic to their hosts; memes like fascism can be toxic to an entire society and can bring it to the brink of war or collapse. Other memes are therapeutic and help people live better lives.

Memes are a technology; just like a computer, they can help you get from intention to actualization. Like every technology from fire to nuclear power, the effects of the technology derive from the intent of the user. Memes exist in a metaphorical ecosystem that seems to mimic nature. Strong memes gain followers and evolve and can rock the planet. I believe if enough people start broadcasting their perspectives, social transformation can't be far behind.

Thanks for buying the book & *happy stickering!*

Srini Kumar
stickernation@gmail.com
http://www.StickerNation.com

P.S. Send us your stickers! And send us photos of how you used this book. Our address: **StickerNation.com, PO Box 2137, Asheville NC 28802 USA**. And if you're on Myspace, visit my profile at www.myspace.com/srini & add me! :)

OPEN ALL CHAKRAS

SAY IT WITH STICKERS * WWW.STICKERNATION.COM ©2006

OPPRESSION IS COWARDICE

SAY IT WITH STICKERS * WWW.STICKERNATION.COM ©2006

ORGASMS ARE GOOD

SAY IT WITH STICKERS * WWW.STICKERNATION.COM ©2006

OVERTHROW SLAVERY

SAY IT WITH STICKERS * WWW.STICKERNATION.COM ©2006

PACIFISM KICKS ASS

SAY IT WITH STICKERS * WWW.STICKERNATION.COM ©2006

Party In Your Head Tonight!

SAY IT WITH STICKERS * WWW.STICKERNATION.COM ©2006

PAY ATTENTION

SAY IT WITH STICKERS * WWW.STICKERNATION.COM ©2006

PEOPLE ARE MIRACLES

SAY IT WITH STICKERS * WWW.STICKERNATION.COM ©2006

PEOPLE BEFORE PROFIT

SAY IT WITH STICKERS * WWW.STICKERNATION.COM ©2006

PERCEPTION IS SELECTIVE

SAY IT WITH STICKERS * WWW.STICKERNATION.COM ©2006

POLICE STATES SUCK

SAY IT WITH STICKERS * WWW.STICKERNATION.COM ©2006

POLLUTION IS PSYCHOTIC

SAY IT WITH STICKERS * WWW.STICKERNATION.COM ©2006

POVERTY SUCKS

SAY IT WITH STICKERS * WWW.STICKERNATION.COM ©2006

POWER TO THE PEOPLE

SAY IT WITH STICKERS * WWW.STICKERNATION.COM ©2006

POWERLESSNESS CORRUPTS

SAY IT WITH STICKERS * WWW.STICKERNATION.COM ©2006

PRACTICE RANDOM ACTS

SAY IT WITH STICKERS * WWW.STICKERNATION.COM ©2006

PREACH AND GET PAID

SAY IT WITH STICKERS * WWW.STICKERNATION.COM ©2006

Prepare to face and defeat the next wave.

SAY IT WITH STICKERS * WWW.STICKERNATION.COM ©2006

PRISONS CAUSE CRIME

SAY IT WITH STICKERS * WWW.STICKERNATION.COM ©2006

PSYCHIATRY IS CRAZY

SAY IT WITH STICKERS * WWW.STICKERNATION.COM ©2006

PUNISH THE PUNDITS

SAY IT WITH STICKERS * WWW.STICKERNATION.COM

QUESTION HEDONISM

SAY IT WITH STICKERS * WWW.STICKERNATION.COM ©200

RACE MIXING IS COOL

SAY IT WITH STICKERS * WWW.STICKERNATION.COM ©200

RAVE AGAINST THE MACHINE

SAY IT WITH STICKERS * WWW.STICKERNATION.COM ©200

READ BANNED BOOKS

SAY IT WITH STICKERS * WWW.STICKERNATION.COM ©200

READING IS SEXY

SAY IT WITH STICKERS * WWW.STICKERNATION.COM ©200

real men dig feminists

SAY IT WITH STICKERS * WWW.STICKERNATION.COM ©200

REBOOT AMERICA

SAY IT WITH STICKERS * WWW.STICKERNATION.COM

REFORM BUSINESS

SAY IT WITH STICKERS * WWW.STICKERNATION.COM ©2006

REFUSE TO LOSE

SAY IT WITH STICKERS * WWW.STICKERNATION.COM ©2006

REJECT RACISM

SAY IT WITH STICKERS * WWW.STICKERNATION.COM ©2006

RELIGION IS DANGEROUS

SAY IT WITH STICKERS * WWW.STICKERNATION.COM ©2006

REMEMBER THE OZONE LAYER

SAY IT WITH STICKERS * WWW.STICKERNATION.COM ©2006

RESCUE THE RIVERS

SAY IT WITH STICKERS * WWW.STICKERNATION.COM ©2006

RESIST DESPAIR

SAY IT WITH STICKERS * WWW.STICKERNATION.COM

RESPECT CERTAIN ELDERS

SAY IT WITH STICKERS * WWW.STICKERNATION.COM ©2006

RETRAIN YOUR BRAIN

SAY IT WITH STICKERS * WWW.STICKERNATION.COM ©2006

REVERSE THE DECAY

SAY IT WITH STICKERS * WWW.STICKERNATION.COM ©2006

SAVE THE HUMANS

SAY IT WITH STICKERS * WWW.STICKERNATION.COM ©2006

SCHOOLS NOT JAILS

SAY IT WITH STICKERS * WWW.STICKERNATION.COM ©2006

SCIENCE WON'T CHANGE YOU

SAY IT WITH STICKERS * WWW.STICKERNATION.COM ©2006

SEIZE LIBERTY

SAY IT WITH STICKERS * WWW.STICKERNATION.COM

THE PRODUCT IS YOU

SAY IT WITH STICKERS * WWW.STICKERNATION.COM
©2006

THE REVOLUTION IS LOVE

SAY IT WITH STICKERS * WWW.STICKERNATION.COM
©2006

THE RICH ARE OBSOLETE

SAY IT WITH STICKERS * WWW.STICKERNATION.COM
©2006

The Right is wrong!

SAY IT WITH STICKERS * WWW.STICKERNATION.COM
©2006

THE SYSTEM'S FRIED

SAY IT WITH STICKERS * WWW.STICKERNATION.COM
©2006

THE WORLD BANK IS TWISTED

SAY IT WITH STICKERS * WWW.STICKERNATION.COM
©2006

THEY COOK THE POLLS

SAY IT WITH STICKERS * WWW.STICKERNATION.COM

THINK AGAIN
SAY IT WITH STICKERS * WWW.STICKERNATION.COM
©2006

THIS ECONOMY SUCKS
SAY IT WITH STICKERS * WWW.STICKERNATION.COM
©2006

THIS ELECTION SUCKS
SAY IT WITH STICKERS * WWW.STICKERNATION.COM
©2006

THIS IS FREEDOM?
SAY IT WITH STICKERS * WWW.STICKERNATION.COM
©2006

THOU SHALT NOT TORTURE
SAY IT WITH STICKERS * WWW.STICKERNATION.COM
©2006

TOMORROW EXISTS TODAY
SAY IT WITH STICKERS * WWW.STICKERNATION.COM
©2006

TOO MUCH PRESSURE
SAY IT WITH STICKERS * WWW.STICKERNATION.COM

TRANSCEND SUFFERING

SAY IT WITH STICKERS * WWW.STICKERNATION.COM
©2006

TRASH YOUR CONDITIONING

SAY IT WITH STICKERS * WWW.STICKERNATION.COM
©2006

TREES ARE PEOPLE TOO

SAY IT WITH STICKERS * WWW.STICKERNATION.COM
©2006

TRUST YOUR LUST

SAY IT WITH STICKERS * WWW.STICKERNATION.COM
©2006

UNDERSTAND THE HOMELESS

SAY IT WITH STICKERS * WWW.STICKERNATION.COM
©2006

UNLEASH INFINITY

SAY IT WITH STICKERS * WWW.STICKERNATION.COM
©2006

USE THE FORCE

SAY IT WITH STICKERS * WWW.STICKERNATION.COM

VOTE FOR ME

SAY IT WITH STICKERS * WWW.STICKERNATION.COM ©2006

Voting Is For Young People

SAY IT WITH STICKERS * WWW.STICKERNATION.COM ©2006

WAR IS CRIMINAL

SAY IT WITH STICKERS * WWW.STICKERNATION.COM ©2006

WARM THE GLOBE

SAY IT WITH STICKERS * WWW.STICKERNATION.COM ©2006

WATER SHOULD BE FREE

SAY IT WITH STICKERS * WWW.STICKERNATION.COM ©2006

WALK YOUR TALK

SAY IT WITH STICKERS * WWW.STICKERNATION.COM ©2006

WE ARE CONNECTED

SAY IT WITH STICKERS * WWW.STICKERNATION.COM ©2006

WE AREN'T FOOLED

SAY IT WITH STICKERS * WWW.STICKERNATION.COM ©2006

WE KNOW IT WAS YOU

SAY IT WITH STICKERS * WWW.STICKERNATION.COM ©2006

WE SHALL OVERCOME

SAY IT WITH STICKERS * WWW.STICKERNATION.COM ©2006

WE WANT THE AIRWAVES

SAY IT WITH STICKERS * WWW.STICKERNATION.COM ©2006

we will build a better tomorrow

SAY IT WITH STICKERS * WWW.STICKERNATION.COM ©2006

WHAT DEMOCRACY?

SAY IT WITH STICKERS * WWW.STICKERNATION.COM ©2006

what does it all mean?

SAY IT WITH STICKERS * WWW.STICKERNATION.COM ©2006

WHAT WOULD GANDHI DO?

SAY IT WITH STICKERS * WWW.STICKERNATION.COM ©2006

WHAT'S STOPPING YOU?

SAY IT WITH STICKERS * WWW.STICKERNATION.COM ©2006

WHERE IS MY MIND?

SAY IT WITH STICKERS * WWW.STICKERNATION.COM ©2006

Whose future is it, anyway?

SAY IT WITH STICKERS * WWW.STICKERNATION.COM ©2006

WHY DOES SCHOOL SUCK?

SAY IT WITH STICKERS * WWW.STICKERNATION.COM ©2006

WHY OBEY MORONS?

SAY IT WITH STICKERS * WWW.STICKERNATION.COM ©2006

WOMEN TAKE OVER

SAY IT WITH STICKERS * WWW.STICKERNATION.COM ©2006

WRITE IT DOWN

SAY IT WITH STICKERS * WWW.STICKERNATION.COM
©2006

YOU ARE NOT WHAT YOU OWN

SAY IT WITH STICKERS * WWW.STICKERNATION.COM
©2006

you are perfection

SAY IT WITH STICKERS * WWW.STICKERNATION.COM
©2006

YOU ARE THE REASON

SAY IT WITH STICKERS * WWW.STICKERNATION.COM
©2006

YOU CAN'T KILL FOR PEACE

SAY IT WITH STICKERS * WWW.STICKERNATION.COM
©2006

YOU DESERVE RESPECT

SAY IT WITH STICKERS * WWW.STICKERNATION.COM
©2006

You LIVE in that head?

YOU MUST WHIP IT
SAY IT WITH STICKERS * WWW.STICKERNATION.COM
©2006

YOU REAP WHAT YOU SOW
SAY IT WITH STICKERS * WWW.STICKERNATION.COM
©2006

YOUR SOUL IS ON A ROLL
SAY IT WITH STICKERS * WWW.STICKERNATION.COM
©2006

YOU'RE ALL SHEEP
SAY IT WITH STICKERS * WWW.STICKERNATION.COM
©2006

you're HEALED!
SAY IT WITH STICKERS * WWW.STICKERNATION.COM
©2006

Your whole system sucks!
SAY IT WITH STICKERS * WWW.STICKERNATION.COM
©2006

your potential is infinite
SAY IT WITH STICKERS * WWW.STICKERNATION.COM
©2006

ADMIT THAT GOTH IS RIDICULOUS

SAY IT WITH STICKERS * WWW.STICKERNATION.COM ©2006

A NATION OF SHEEP WILL BE RULED BY PIGS

SAY IT WITH STICKERS * WWW.STICKERNATION.COM ©2006

APPRECIATE THE IMPLICATIONS

SAY IT WITH STICKERS * WWW.STICKERNATION.COM ©2006

ASK ME ABOUT MY CONSPIRACY THEORY

SAY IT WITH STICKERS * WWW.STICKERNATION.COM ©2006

AUTONOMY IS THE ANSWER

SAY IT WITH STICKERS * WWW.STICKERNATION.COM

BETTER THINK OF YOUR FUTURE

SAY IT WITH STICKERS * WWW.STICKERNATION.COM
©2006

BEWARE OF IDIOTS POSING AS KINGS

SAY IT WITH STICKERS * WWW.STICKERNATION.COM
©2006

COMBAT THE RACIST INFRASTRUCTURE

DON'T EAT YOUR SOUL TO FILL YOUR BELLY

SAY IT WITH STICKERS * WWW.STICKERNATION.COM ©2006

DON'T GET BLOOD ON MY FLAG

SAY IT WITH STICKERS * WWW.STICKERNATION.COM ©2006

DON'T HATE THE PLAYER HATE THE GAME

SAY IT WITH STICKERS * WWW.STICKERNATION.COM ©2006

DON'T LET OUR YOUTH GO TO WASTE

SAY IT WITH STICKERS * WWW.STICKERNATION.COM ©2006

EDUCATION IS EVERYWHERE

SAY IT WITH STICKERS * WWW.STICKERNATION.COM ©2006

ENDURANCE IS EVERYTHING

SAY IT WITH STICKERS * WWW.STICKERNATION.COM ©2006

EVERY COMMODITY YOU PRODUCE FEEDS THE BELLIES OF THE PIGS THAT EXPLOIT US

SAY IT WITH STICKERS * WWW.STICKERNATION.COM ©2006

EVERYTHING IS PHENOMENAL

SAY IT WITH STICKERS * WWW.STICKERNATION.COM 2006

EVOLVE

SAY IT WITH STICKERS * WWW.STICKERNATION.COM ©2006

FACTORY SMOKE IS NOT PROGRESS

SAY IT WITH STICKERS * WWW.STICKERNATION.COM

FAKE NEWS
GET OFF THE AIR

SAY IT WITH STICKERS * WWW.STICKERNATION.COM
©2006

FOCUS

SAY IT WITH STICKERS * WWW.STICKERNATION.COM
©2006

FUNDAMENTALISM
IS WRONG

SAY IT WITH STICKERS * WWW.STICKERNATION.COM
©2006

FREEDOM
IS THE ATTITUDE

SAY IT WITH STICKERS * WWW.STICKERNATION.COM
©2006

genetic engineering:
it's what's for dinner

SAY IT WITH STICKERS * WWW.STICKERNATION.COM

I AM THE CENTER OF THE UNIVERSE

SAY IT WITH STICKERS * WWW.STICKERNATION.COM
©200

i don't understand what i'm saying

SAY IT WITH STICKERS * WWW.STICKERNATION.COM
©200

IF YOU ENJOY FREEDOM YOU BETTER SPEAK UP

SAY IT WITH STICKERS * WWW.STICKERNATION.COM
©200

I THINK THEREFORE I'M AWESOME

SAY IT WITH STICKERS * WWW.STICKERNATION.COM
©200

JOIN US

SAY IT WITH STICKERS * WWW.STICKERNATION.COM

LOVE

SAY IT WITH STICKERS * WWW.STICKERNATION.COM
©2006

MORE UNITY
IN THE COMMUNITY

SAY IT WITH STICKERS * WWW.STICKERNATION.COM
©2006

My dad's a cop too, couldja let me go now?

SAY IT WITH STICKERS * WWW.STICKERNATION.COM
©2006

Only by breaking free of psychic constraints can we hope to become unique individuals.

SAY IT WITH STICKERS * WWW.STICKERNATION.COM
©2006

PEACE

SAY IT WITH STICKERS * WWW.STICKERNATION.COM
©2006

PLEASE DON'T START WORLD WAR III

SAY IT WITH STICKERS * WWW.STICKERNATION.COM ©2006

pledge allegiance to the entire world

SAY IT WITH STICKERS * WWW.STICKERNATION.COM ©2006

PRODUCE OR BE CONSUMED

SAY IT WITH STICKERS * WWW.STICKERNATION.COM ©2006

Protest Slave Labor At Your Local Mall

SAY IT WITH STICKERS * WWW.STICKERNATION.COM ©2006

RACIAL PREJUDICE IS MENTAL ILLNESS

SAY IT WITH STICKERS * WWW.STICKERNATION.COM

REAL LEADERS AVOID FOLLOWERS

SAY IT WITH STICKERS * WWW.STICKERNATION.COM ©200

RESISTANCE IS NOT FUTILE

SAY IT WITH STICKERS * WWW.STICKERNATION.COM ©200

RIDDIM IS THE VOICE OF JAH

SAY IT WITH STICKERS * WWW.STICKERNATION.COM ©200

RIGHT-WING RADIO: THE VOICE OF SATAN

SAY IT WITH STICKERS * WWW.STICKERNATION.COM ©200

RISE ABOVE

SAY IT WITH STICKERS * WWW.STICKERNATION.COM

SEPARATE
CHURCH AND STATE

SAY IT WITH STICKERS * WWW.STICKERNATION.COM
©2006

SIMPLIFY

SAY IT WITH STICKERS * WWW.STICKERNATION.COM
©2006

SMART KIDS
NOT SMART BOMBS

TAXATION WITHOUT REPRESENTATION IS TYRANNY

SAY IT WITH STICKERS * WWW.STICKERNATION.COM
©2006

THE CRAP IN THE AIR WILL MESS UP YOUR FACE

SAY IT WITH STICKERS * WWW.STICKERNATION.COM
©2006

THE GUITAR IS MIGHTIER THAN THE SWORD

SAY IT WITH STICKERS * WWW.STICKERNATION.COM
©2006

the ideology of organized religion is social control

SAY IT WITH STICKERS * WWW.STICKERNATION.COM
©2006

THE ROAD TO HELL IS PAVED WITH LANDMINES

SAY IT WITH STICKERS * WWW.STICKERNATION.COM
©2006

the universe is a
computer simulation

SAY IT WITH STICKERS * WWW.STICKERNATION.COM
©2006

THE WAR ON DRUGS
IS STUPID

SAY IT WITH STICKERS * WWW.STICKERNATION.COM
©2006

THE WORKING CLASS
IS EXPLOITED

SAY IT WITH STICKERS * WWW.STICKERNATION.COM
©2006

THE WORLD IS
DRUNK ON OIL

SAY IT WITH STICKERS * WWW.STICKERNATION.COM
©2006

TIMELESS

SAY IT WITH STICKERS * WWW.STICKERNATION.COM

VIOLENCE AGAINST WOMEN WILL NOT BE TOLERATED

SAY IT WITH STICKERS * WWW.STICKERNATION.COM ©2006

WAKE UP

SAY IT WITH STICKERS * WWW.STICKERNATION.CO ©200

WEIRD CHEMICALS ARE EVERYWHERE

SAY IT WITH STICKERS * WWW.STICKERNATION.CO ©200

WHAT A DRAG IT IS GETTING SOLD

SAY IT WITH STICKERS * WWW.STICKERNATION.CO ©20

What is stopping you from doing something so cool that it renders you IMMORTAL?

what you are
is what you decide to be

SAY IT WITH STICKERS * WWW.STICKERNATION.COM
©2006

when i hit the drum
you shake the booty

SAY IT WITH STICKERS * WWW.STICKERNATION.COM
©2006

WORD

SAY IT WITH STICKERS * WWW.STICKERNATION.COM
©2006

YES I CAN

SAY IT WITH STICKERS * WWW.STICKERNATION.COM
©2006

You are stupid and evil and do not know that you are stupid and evil.

SAY IT WITH STICKERS * WWW.STICKERNATION.COM

YOU CALL *THAT*
"CONSERVATIVE"?

SAY IT WITH STICKERS * WWW.STICKERNATION.COM
©2006

YOU RULE

SAY IT WITH STICKERS * WWW.STICKERNATION.COM
©2006

YOUR BRAIN
IS OUR DOMAIN

SAY IT WITH STICKERS * WWW.STICKERNATION.COM
©2006

YOUR DATABASE
DOESN'T KNOW ME

SAY IT WITH STICKERS * WWW.STICKERNATION.COM
©2006

ZERO TOLERANCE
FOR INTOLERANCE

SAY IT WITH STICKERS * WWW.STICKERNATION.COM
©2006

EVERYTHING YOU KNOW IS
WRONG

©MMVI disinformation® ♀ www.disinfo.com

YOU ARE BEING
LIED TO

©MMVI disinformation® ♀ www.disinfo.com

TURN OFF YOUR MIND

©MMVI disinformation® ♀ www.disinfo.com

GENERATION HEX

©MMVI disinformation® ♀ www.disinfo.com

EVERYTHING YOU KNOW ABOUT
SEX IS WRONG

©MMVI disinformation® ♀ www.disinfo.com

"Have a good time, ALL the time." —*Viv Savage (keyboards),* This Is Spinal Tap

There are more ideas to conquer than there are stars in the night sky. I'm going to try and get to all of them.

"Those who would sacrifice liberty for security deserve neither." —*Ben Franklin*

"Reality is that which, when you stop believing in it, doesn't go away." —*Philip K. Dick*

Technology has made it easy to sleep through life. Virtual realities projected on TV can make *real* reality seem trivial.

"It's so very lonely, you're two thousand light years from home..." —*The Rolling Stones*

"The future of the book is the blurb." -*Marshall McLuhan*

The question, as Rodney King posed it after the 1992 Los Angeles riots, is "Can't we all just get along?"

I want to inherit a world that we can work with, not a world out of control.

The BOREDOM and IRRELEVANCE of most work makes us dread rather than relish the passage of time on the job.

The segregation of society extends up the class hierarchy as well as down. Yuppies are the "Outer Party" Orwell envisioned.

My hope is that you're not yet deadened by the conspiracy of dunces that dominate the mainstream media.

It is very easy for the "progressive" side of the political spectrum to descend into bitterness. Luckily there's a cure!

Get a new angle to help you navigate the complex interaction of human design and its artifacts with the environment.

"The gun industry has long known its practices aid criminal access to guns yet has done nothing about it." —*Joshua Horowitz*
Executive Director for the Coalition to Stop Gun Violence: http://www.csgv.org/

The definition of "wealth" ought to be expanded to mean something deeper than currency and financial assets.

Monoculture has constrained our domain of relevant activities. We identify with what we own, not what we could become.

The right to contraception is *obviously* a human right. It was *illegal* for single women to use the Pill in the USA until *1972!*
source: http://www.metafilter.com/mefi/41880

The "code of law" ought to be OPEN-SOURCED! Twisted forces are shaping the legislative agenda. We demand a recount!

Counterculture is a cartoon. The punks need to switch tactics. I wasn't in the pit when the rulebooks were handed out.

The record industry will ultimately benefit from the Internet's impact. They tried to stop the cassette tape too. Didn't work.
meme engineered by Epitonic.com

The rhythms and melodies and the life experiences that music accompanies frame the lyrics for instant recall.

"You have to realize every myth is a metaphor."—*Screeching Weasel*

Your taxes work in bizarre and even *sinister* ways. Aristocrats battle bureaucrats in the legislature; the people pay the price.

Media programming technology and consolidation hasn't smashed independent publishing; it has only firmed up our resolve.

Isn't there a way of looking at language as "code" and of certain linguistic or ideological tactics as "functions"?

Tsunamis, earthquakes, famines and killer storms. Maybe the planet is trying to tell us something.

During anti-Nazi riots in post-unification Germany in 1992, I witnessed the damage done by ideological pattern manipulation.

The stickers in this book are audience-specific. I know from the fact that you're reading this that I endorse your mission.

If you get a feeling that someone you meet is a jerk, odds are everyone else feels the same way about them too.

State your inability to fret to the world and maybe the world will stop handing you reasons to do so.

Bizarre images flash across the television news demanding that we hate or be hated. These values may bury humanity.

Archetypes lead to behaviors. Behaviors lead to circumstances. Circumstances lead to decisions. Decisions lead to evolution.

"I Like What I am Playing and I Don't Want to Improve." —*Mike Korzek (song title)*
http://www.gloriousnoise.com/articles/2004/korzek-10-13.php
Phony DJmania has bitten the dust. Last night a DJ shopped for records and practiced smooth moves in front of a mirror.
http://www.salon.com/ent/music/feature/2000/03/14/machinesoul/index.html

LIVE IT UP
LIVE LONG AND PROSPER
LIVE THE CHAOS
LOGIC IS YOUR FRIEND
LOOK ALIVE
LOST IN SPACE
LOUDER THAN THE MEDIA

LOVE IS THE ANSWER
MAKE IT STOP
MAKE LOVE NOT WORK
MAKE YUPPIES REPENT
MASS MEDIA MAKES MORONS
MAYBE PARTYING WILL HELP
MEET US IN ORBIT

MELT ALL GUNS
MONEY ISN'T WEALTH
Money Is Not Our God
MORE ORGASMS FEWER KIDS
MORE POINTLESS LAWS
MOSH CLOCKWISE
MP3 IS NOT A CRIME

music keeps me sane
MY BRAIN HURTS
MY GOVERNMENT IS NUTS
MY TECHNOLOGY RULES
MY WORD IS MY BOND
NATURE IS PISSED
NAZIS ARE PATHETIC

NEVER GIVE UP
NO ROOM FOR PHONIES
NO WORRIES
NOBODY HATES YOU
ONE THING LEADS TO ANOTHER
ONLY GOD CAN JUDGE ME
ooh! ooh! can I be a DJ too? please?

OPEN ALL CHAKRAS — We have chakras (energy centers) that extend from the tops of our heads and can be flung all around the known universe.

OPPRESSION IS COWARDICE — "Violence is the last refuge of the incompetent." —Isaac Asimov, Foundation

ORGASMS ARE GOOD — "Genital gratification and the avoidance of compulsory sex-morality [is] the key to avoiding a pathological society."
Alex Burns writing about the work of Wilhelm Reich: http://www.disinfo.com/archive/pages/dossier/id217/pg1/

OVERTHROW SLAVERY — Workers worldwide shackle themselves to the engine of global capitalism. Did you know M&M's are made with slave labor?
http://www.globalexchange.org/campaigns/fairtrade/cocoa/

PACIFISM KICKS ASS — Pacifism is not passivity. Pacifism is a moral stance requiring courage and commitment.

Party In Your Head Tonight! — Do we really have control of what's in our minds? Freud didn't think so. But maybe that's OK!

PAY ATTENTION — Invest your attention wisely. Mastering your attention and keeping it under your control is critical.

PEOPLE ARE MIRACLES — The complexity of the systems that sustain our lives from within and without is astonishing.

PEOPLE BEFORE PROFIT — Social/cultural concerns, the welfare of workers, economic and environmental ecology - all subordinate to the bottom line.

PERCEPTION IS SELECTIVE — We live in a turbulent ocean of ideas and concepts. Most information varies widely in utility, accuracy, and perspective.

POLICE STATES SUCK — "Once the State has granted itself power to take away a right, it can continue revoking that right from whomever it pleases." —Russ Kick
http://www.disinfo.com/archive/pages/article/id1420/pg1/

POLLUTION IS PSYCHOTIC — ExxonMobil has spent millions on junk science groups to lie about global warming. They must have mansions on the Moon.
http://action.truemajority.org/campaign/Exxon

POVERTY SUCKS — The gap between the richest and poorest continues to widen. Millions are sinking in the quicksand of the global economy.

POWER TO THE PEOPLE — Strategists develop quick responses to the population's resistance to their hegemony, but technological diffusion is faster.

POWERLESSNESS CORRUPTS — People are missing out on the joy of participatory democracy. The folks working with Martin Luther King had a great time!

PRACTICE RANDOM ACTS — A pithier restatement of a common hippy sticker slogan. The irony: if you practice, they aren't random acts... or are they?

PREACH AND GET PAID — Can you see where your own ideas might fit into the world? No? Well let's set you up with a suburban megachurch then!

Prepare to face and defeat the next wave. — The ocean's waves resemble our biorhythms. The best way to master the waves is to get yourself a surfboard.

PRISONS CAUSE CRIME — I'm not sure that incarcerating criminals together is a swift idea. Unless of course you're in the market for cheap labor.

PSYCHIATRY IS CRAZY — Pharmaceutical firms have expert salesmen who pose as shamans. The very names of the drugs sound like evil spells.

PUNISH THE PUNDITS — Thinktanks weave cushions of words to soften their client politicians' harsh policies and disguise their true allegiances.

QUESTION HEDONISM — People may seek to maximize their fun, but they always seem to run up against a limit. Why not take a saner approach?

RACE MIXING IS COOL — Our DNA is blending and insecure idiots don't like it. Race rules for relationships are hatred institutionalized as "morality."

RAVE AGAINST THE MACHINE — A DJ once told me "rave needs more punk rock." Underground music needs to be as revolutionary as the vinyl discs it spins.

READ BANNED BOOKS — Banned books contain alien ideascapes. When the monoculture bans books it's tantamount to a recommendation.

READING IS SEXY — Reading represents a symbiosis, or merging, of the individual with words. When we read we are in another dimension.

real men dig feminists — Feminism was established to give women access to the code on which this society is run.

REBOOT AMERICA — How about a new "special interest group" that cares about the spirit of democracy and does everything it can to restore it?

REFORM BUSINESS — Tons of money for capitalists to make in the world. Why destroy rivers and forests? Businesses owe their existence to you!

REFUSE TO LOSE — You have to accommodate risk in your plans. If you anticipate your obstacles your determination will help you defeat them.

REJECT RACISM — Do racists really think of their skin color as their defining characteristic? The pitiful lives they must lead!

RELIGION IS DANGEROUS — If there is a God, every single one of us is an authorized representative. Organized religion generally doesn't see it that way.

REMEMBER THE OZONE LAYER — The Battle of Armageddon is swirling across the stratosphere. Which side are you on?

RESCUE THE RIVERS — Many towns were founded on rivers that have now turned toxic. We NEED clean rivers, but not enough people seem to care.

RESIST DESPAIR — You are never the first person to have gone through your particular pain. The pain washes in waves across generations.

Many historical exemplars of "gravitas" have started wars and tortured people. Age doesn't equal wisdom; it *implies* it.

Growing up we're told to behave or not to behave in specific ways. Ideally that's when you discover The Book of the SubGenius.
http://www.subgenius.com
Develop friendly messaging tactics that might stimulate somebody boneheaded to change their mind.

The genius 1981 video game *Defender* invited players to duck into hyperspace and rescue humans captured by mutant aliens.

Schools and jails are both state monopolies with locked-in customers. The resemblance ought to end there but it doesn't.

Fire can cook food or destroy a city. Our technology gives us great power, but wisdom isn't always included in the manual.

The only *real* rights are rights you *use*. Freedom isn't just abstract; it's an energy in the moment that changes your approach.

We live in a Permanent Autonomous Zone; we ARE free, but economic/cultural/political traps make us forget to BE free.

When we were in high school we had "sex ed" that conveniently avoided any acknowledgement of FUN.

Words disappear but ideas and emotions are transferred anyway. The sounds of the natural world fill the air. Shhhhh.

Dividing the sexes is a critical precondition for ideological control. The world is off-balance until we make sexism obsolete.

Memes flash across our culture like amber waves of pain. Seize the high ground and hang on!

Breathing clear air is a human right. Smog covers many modern cities like a thick blanket of post-industrial remorse.

One determined individual can overturn an entire conspiracy. Secrets are more valuable than Persian Gulf mineral rights.

Why is there so much hunger in the modern world? Wealth is like blood; if it doesn't circulate, the entire system fails.

Media images cause insecure people to strike poses that resemble them. Imitation is the sincerest form of idiocy.

Break out of the cubicle farm and roam free on the plains. Toss your inbox in the air, let out a wild whoop, and run! FAST!

Imagine if kids could vote and were no longer second class citizens. When students speak, the future is channelled today.

The systems on which civilization runs are messing up the planet. Choices made long ago should not be fixed forever.

Time passes. Your fortunes, those of your friends and family, and verily the entire world changes in infinite ways every moment.

All language is a realignment of consciousness. When we speak in any given moment we participate in it.

Remember to detect the subliminal forces that influence your surroundings. There are "hidden messages" everywhere.

In free markets the benefits of production are distributed unevenly. The rich find loopholes to make sure it stays that way.

Protest is an integral part of democracy. It is unlikely those policing these events think about what they're attacking.

With few exceptions, roles women play on television reinforce passive/negative stereotypes that bleed into the real world.

Prejudice splits humanity apart for no reason. Definitions work (somewhat) for words, but not for entire classes of *people*.

Did God tell us to chop down all the trees and enslave the Third World? Did God demand that we develop biowarfare?

Without trust we all become paranoid. Invest in relationships where distrust could not possibly become an issue.

Optimism may be out of vogue in these troubled times. I still can't help it. The future is too interesting for me to give up.

Politicians read speeches and toss the index cards in the trash. The directive is what matters; the words a mere device.

Give this sticker to your favorite technology buff and maybe they'll invent something super cool for the rest of us.

Routes for international shipping are opening across the Arctic Circle as the ice melts. Ecodisaster is an investment opportunity.

The internet is sociology on steroids. Information is our mental DNA, and you can watch it mutate online.

Creativity is a whirling vortex of ideas, a hurricane uprooting the structures we previously had imposed on our thoughts.

Like the Internet but in the material world, stickers break the monopoly that mass media pretends it still holds.

RESPECT CERTAIN ELDERS
RETRAIN YOUR BRAIN
REVERSE THE DECAY
SAVE THE HUMANS
SCHOOLS NOT JAILS
SCIENCE WON'T CHANGE YOU
SEIZE LIBERTY

SET ME FREE
SEX TOYS ROCK
SHHHHHH. LISTEN.
SMASH PATRIARCHY
SOCIETY IS SPASTIC
SPARE THE AIR
SPIN WON'T HIDE A LIE

STAMP OUT HUNGER
STOP FAKING IT
STOP LIVING LIKE VEAL
STUDENT POWER
SUPPORT SUSTAINABLE SYSTEMS
take nothing for granted
TALK NERDY TO ME

TAO IS ETERNAL
TAX THE RICH
TEAR GAS SUCKS
TELEVISION IS SEXIST
TERMINATE PREJUDICE
THANK GOD I'M AGNOSTIC
thank you for not screwing me over

The Best Is Yet To Come
the ends justify the memes
the geeks shall inherit the earth
THE ICE CAPS ARE MELTING
THE INTERNET CHANGED MY LIFE
THE ONLY CONSTANT IS CHANGE
THE STREETS ARE ALIVE

THE PRODUCT IS YOU	There is a limited supply of human attention. The product market demands more and will resort to anything to keep it.
THE REVOLUTION IS LOVE	In many minds the concept of "revolution" is fraught with violence. A revolution happens every day the Earth spins.
THE RICH ARE OBSOLETE	Culture can be shaped from a laptop. The monopoly the rich once held in media power is eroding. (Has eroded?)
The Right is wrong!	Much focus is spent in ideological circles defining "us" versus "them." These circles must open to wider perspectives.
THE SYSTEM'S FRIED	Thinking about "systems" makes more sense than thinking only of discrete elements. Most people do not think this way.
THE WORLD BANK IS TWISTED	"Not one country has successfully developed thanks to the World Bank's system..." —Nick Mamatas http://www.disinfo.com/archive/pages/dossier/id337/pg1/index.html
THEY COOK THE POLLS	Politicians use polls to determine what to say on the stump, which then affects the media, which shapes our opinions.

THINK AGAIN	People resist new information. We reject ideas that don't "fit" the framework that we cling to for our bearings.
THIS ECONOMY SUCKS	"Free enterprise" should not mean government subsidy. The modern economy has evolved from feudalism, but not much.
THIS ELECTION SUCKS	Incompetent candidates get elected through database marketing, mudslinging and photo-ops with religious leaders.
THIS IS FREEDOM?	The marketing of "freedom" is a political gimmick, because psychological methods of control are sold to us as "information."
THOU SHALT NOT TORTURE	Deny any possible benefit from the use of torture as an interrogation tactic.
TOMORROW EXISTS TODAY	Building blocks for the future are all around us. Peer into the future by means of a bold and original view of the present.
TOO MUCH PRESSURE	The stress of civilized life keeps us "busy," but is it really helping? There are solutions to stress in every group of friends.

TRANSCEND SUFFERING	There are times to withdraw, attack, delay, and accelerate. There really isn't much time left to suffer.
TRASH YOUR CONDITIONING	Somehow we get told where on the totem pole we belong and we tend to stay there for the rest of our lives.
TREES ARE PEOPLE TOO	Imagine if trees could vote too! "So the maples formed a union/And demanded equal rights...." —Rush
TRUST YOUR LUST	If orgone energy is emanating from within you, that is going to be your priority, so you might as well roll with it.
UNDERSTAND THE HOMELESS	Those most victimized by modern macroeconomics can probably tell the rest of us a lot about its flaws.
UNLEASH INFINITY	The potential of your network isn't tapped. These skills and resources only require your coordination to reach the stars.
USE THE FORCE	Destiny has a shape; it has texture and rhythm and harmony. The future is in the hands of those who choose to shape it.

VOTE FOR ME	In a "democracy" the "people" are supposed to rule. You're elected; now what?
Voting Is For Young People	Our generation will break the hex of hegemony in the collective discourse. Maybe we can skip Armageddon.
WAR IS CRIMINAL	It's convenient to label orgies of murder and rape with the moniker "war." Such a simple label for a horror so complex.
WARM THE GLOBE	Surf's up! The mechanisms of modern production run counter to eco-logic. Grab a board and don't forget the sunblock!
WATER SHOULD BE FREE	"The conglomerate doubled and tripled prices. Many impoverished people suddenly couldn't afford the essence of life." Robert Sterling on the World Bank in Bolivia: http://www.disinfo.com/archive/pages/dossier/id428/pg1/index.html
WALK YOUR TALK	You can say you want change, but this sticker will make sure you keep working for it.
WE ARE CONNECTED	Every human adds to the value of your own life. Beneficial network effects are the foundation of our prosperity.

WE AREN'T FOOLED	Vast sums of money build powerful media edifices to massage the truth into a shape compatible with the needs of capital.
WE KNOW IT WAS YOU	If democracy is the rule of the State by the People, we get the leaders we deserve. Let's start "deserving" reform!
WE SHALL OVERCOME	You might be broke in dollars but rich in MOVES.
WE WANT THE AIRWAVES	The people are the future of broadcasting. The history of all hitherto existing society is the history of media monopoly.
we will build a better tomorrow	The effects of a technology derive from the intent of those who wield it. The Free Internet is the future of broadcasting!
WHAT DEMOCRACY?	Violence, war, money, secrets, conspiracies, and propaganda set manipulating the Will of the People as a primary target.
what does it all mean?	"Difficult preaching is Posdnuos' pleasure/Pleasure and preaching starts in the heart." —De La Soul

"First they ignore you, then they laugh at you, then they fight you, then you win." —*Mahatma Gandhi*

We must commit to placing our hearts and our creative energies in opposition to what we see as wrong in society.

Propaganda imprints in our minds new methods to analyze the world and pretend that we thought about it ourselves.

Roles are assigned us in gradeschool based on our supposed "intelligence" and we tend to stay in those roles forever.

Public education is running on an old operating system. Maybe we can improve its quality with *less* school, not more.

People on both sides of any argument can be idiots. The idiots always shout loudest. Don't let them speak for you.

The War of the Sexes is headed for a stalemate. Women have made huge contributions to society; they should get to run it!

After conversations ideas may be lost forever. If you write them down, it's like tucking away money under the bed for a rainy day.

Don't be possessed by your possessions. The objects in your orbit may be nothing more than space junk.

Even our flaws are perfect. Well before we were born, circumstances conspired to generate us.

All of history exists to fuel the hope that you will use what you have learned and acquired in unexpected, original ways.

The rhetoric of war bristles with justifications for bloodshed. The victims are generally not part of the discussion.

We hope for collaboration in our society. We are only limited by our mutual respect. We should be quicker to convey it.

Many stories from the fringe are destined to begin with "so this one time at Burning Man..." This is one of them.

Obstacles exist to make our efforts tougher. Sincere effort is its own reward, but when you're stuck, kick it up a notch.

"According to the Vedas, if we sow goodness, we will reap goodness; if we sow evil, we will reap evil." —*Wikipedia*
http://en.wikipedia.org/wiki/Karma

YOU have the skills to become a transformational organism, a catalyst for the potential that's all around you.

Isn't this concept spread through organized religion? That people are sheep to be guided by authority lest they be "lost"?

I choose to believe that stickers change reality. I am aware this belief is quixotic, but what if I'm right?

You can best oppose ugly systems by designing and implementing better ones and persuading good people to sign up.

Each of us can be innovators. You pay attention to your life; that attention is an investment. Your investment will pay off.

The variety of subcultures that branched out from "punk rock" is one crazy ecosystem. After Joy Division what's the point?

Orwell's *Animal Farm* allegorically implies that we're dupes of coordinated manipulators, letting our rights decay out of fear or ignorance. "Four legs bad, two legs better" bleat the sheep, and the pigs learn how to walk like men and carry whips.

You can take any scenario and chart out different outcomes; you know, "this is the best-case scenario" and "this is the worst-case scenario." Why were we never taught *any* planning concepts in our twelve years of school?

"Conspiracy theory" is a biased label that lets people with a hegemonic (e.g. "mainstream") worldview characterize and caricature people who have uncovered information about groups that use devious tactics to shape human destiny.

You can't create more happiness with technology alone. You've got to change the way people think and act. *Autonomy* is a person's ability to make independent choices. Without truly distinct and innovative options, "choice" is meaningless.

When we make our decisions (or have them made for us) we set a trajectory for our destiny to play out. This is "karma" in a nutshell. Many of us act out superficial roles rather than developing our unique productive potentials.

Democracy paints a glossy veneer of equality and populism over the machinations of whoever can manipulate their way through election season. Once a "mandate" is "clearly established" the aristocratic tendencies of rule can re-emerge.

The logic of modern political and economic dominion carries the DNA of imperialism. It took years before MTV deigned to play videos of black artists. The system that made slaves of millions of Africans for centuries has persisted to the present.

We are literally scarring the earth with mining and drilling operations to get at the molecular deposits of gold that remain. Huge corporations are transforming entire islands worth of solid rock into billions of tons of cyanide-laced slurry.

Money is no *object*. It's a surreal force that captures our imaginations. The spreadsheets of corporate planners are rejected until they show an acceptable rate of return. The orgy of infinite growth may result in a nasty hangover.

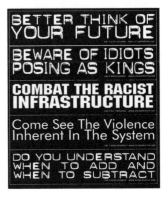

In my cryptic realignment of language "soul" is a metaphor for *potential*. We trade our potential to gain strength or resources, but we may stripmine our potential to satisfy pressing economic needs. This sacrifice can only yield shallow benefits.

Foreign policy cannot be ruled by the paranoid. Fictionalized nightmare battle scenarios zap the common sense from the heads of officials who see their power as a right and not a duty. The profitability of war to certain firms is sickening.

There is no substitute for the stimulus of an active opponent. When systems yield poor results or get hijacked by those of ill intent, fix the system, not the symptom. Address the root causes of the recurring failures. Winners don't take it personally.

The long-term view of the potential of kids doesn't jibe with how our society generally treats them. When young people are given tools, they use them in surprising ways. The future of the world is in good hands, but let's teach them how to build.

If we live in an information universe, then why not grab some and turn that into an education? I learned how to use computers by myself, as did many of you. I've gotten a lot out of school, sure, but why stop learning? EVER?

"Good luck" is often actually the result of a long period of unrewarded effort. Time makes our efforts honest. Focus on your power to take pressure and the patience to watch solutions emerge. Never underestimate the power of an allnighter.

When we produce in conjunction with work, we support a system of production that is far larger than we can perceive. The products that surround us at large retail establishments are an advertisement for a prosperity that's based on exploitation. *This sticker is a merger of two lines from the excellent Richard Linklater movie Slacker - check it out!*

Stickers jut out into the real world. Most books (and I love books) are meant to be read by individuals and placed back on a bookshelf. This is a book full of tiny invasions of the material world. *Your reaction is my art;* the stickers just a catalyst.

The "Tree of Life" branches out from our ancestors. DNA is a song that echoes back to the primordial swamp. The rhythms of reproduction are eternal and we are related to the entire living world. Evolution never ended; mutants rule the Earth!

The Industrial Revolution spread faster than the knowledge that pollution was bad for human beings. In the 1900s cities BOASTED about their smog as proof of their economic vitality. The goals of human productivity ought to include survival.

There is a reason that they call television content "programming"; when our skepticism has been overwhelmed by spectacle, deafened by loud proclamations and the method acting of anchors feigning objectivity, our own judgment becomes faulty.

Cultural choices have replaced political choices. We spend our energy differentiating ourselves culturally; political apathy is inevitable. Political consciousness involves studying, evaluating, planning and acting; it's all about staying focused!

Religious fundamentalism is borne of alienation, not communion. The fundamentalist views the manifest world as against their beliefs, but faith must reflect the real world or anything goes. Using "doublethink" to bridge this gap is unethical.

Be a vaccine against fascism. Inoculate your friends against the toxic substance of oppression. They will develop their own resistance. Antitoxins will fight and neutralize the poisons, developing their immunity to similar future toxins.

One of the more troubling developments of modern technology is the pace at which we are manipulating our own food supply. Large agricultural conglomerates just don't think Mother Nature is efficient enough to match their targets.

Since none of us can perceive the whole universe, we all experience *portions* of the universe selected by our circumstances or by our decisions; elements of our universe are either thrust upon us, or perceived or ignored according to our priorities.

Things are rarely as they seem. The communications we convey are layered with noise and twists of perspective. How often are we truly conscious of what we say? The scenario and one's audience inspire all kinds of semantic contortions.

Democracy only works in a context of some kind of social order and collective common sense. Elections and policy discussions mean little to a population with no power. Let's redefine power to include our capacity to transmit our thoughts.

I represent the power to perceive and evaluate my own destiny. I want you to feel the same way. I know that I can create and have others care. "To explain, I was meant to exercise this brain."—*Stereolab*

Power to the dissatisfied! The dissatisfied see this world correctly - as not perfect yet. The world is full of potential for positive change. The modifications you want to see to society become *inevitable* once enough people demand them.

"Survival of the fittest" is no way to run a planet. Love shapes every life, from womb to tomb, and the more love we find, the more we give. An endless, self-replenishing resource, love is within everyone's reach and as it spreads, things *change*.

If we work together as a *team*, the work gets EASY and FUN. "Nothing in the universe can resist the cumulative ardor of a sufficiently large number of enlightened minds working together in organized groups." —*Teilhard de Chardin*

The scenario: getting pulled over by a policeman for speeding. This sticker: gets a chuckle out of the authority figure, thus interfering with the usual protocol of interaction. Positional power ebbs away and you get away without a ticket... yeah!

You have control over the dynamics of the processes in your life. You become more persuasive when you pioneer new approaches to the various scenarios that you face. This sense of breakthrough will permeate everything you do.

Peace is a lot more to me than the opposite of war. During moments of serenity the *conceptual* nature of reality becomes more flexible and I get ideas on how to tweak and optimize my experience. Peace is always a winning strategy.

Militaries the world over have worked hard to create an atmosphere of antagonism crackling with pointless violence, because it makes their own guilt that much easier to hide. "An eye for an eye makes everybody blind." —*Mahatma Gandhi*

We may at any time receive information that profoundly alters our universe and the way we behave within it. Maybe Marx was onto something when he spoke of the "withering away of the State." Not a new world order, but a new world SPIRIT.

The demands of work are ever-increasing; we have little consolidated attention remaining to think of our society and the forces that shape it. Democracy is a privilege of those who can afford to run for office. Many of the poor don't even vote.

For decades corporations thought nothing of importing goods manufactured through human bondage. Pressure from activist groups has been incredibly effective in forcing these companies to re-evaluate their supply "chains."

Stereotypes make life a lot easier for the simpleminded. Racist minds can't bear to confront their own anger, so they project it at their perceived adversaries. "If we're scared of one another, we must be scared of ourselves." —*Operation Ivy*

Decry the arrogance of leaders who glorify imperialism and the despoilment of nature. The real leaders in this world lead by example, not shows of authority or dominion. Surround a person with followers, that will not make them worthy or wise.

Despite the indications that play across financial media about the relative strength of the economy, notice how we work ever-longer hours at more difficult jobs for lower pay with fewer benefits, less security, and stupider bosses?

We experience music as a powerful synaesthesia that sometimes gets write access to our memory. The rhythms and melodies and the life experiences that music accompanies frame the lyrics for instant recall.

"We have to invade everybody!" "Make birth control illegal!" "Censor rap music and video games!" "Healthcare needs to be more like the stock market!" News flash to bozo: just because idiots think you're "convincing," doesn't make it the truth.

The bugs define the system. Troubleshooting your situation is not difficult. It's easy to change your life; all you have to do is wake up one day and say "I'm going to start working out" or "I'm going to quit that job." It's a lot harder to stick with it.

The rules along which crazies from the clergy would have us live are absurd. They can only be foisted upon us by the State. To augment religious and moral rules with the law is the fantasy of every controlling lunatic in organized religion.

There are few systems that can't be improved. If you focus on the areas of complication in your life and find simple, consistent solutions, you can form better habits and become more effective. This is obvious, but this sticker is a reminder.

When the dust clears we find that the bombs our war machines have hurled are a lot less intelligent than we're told they are. The United States has a "Department of Defense" that does nothing to defend Americans; it's just plain *offensive*.

Who on TV is in debt? What sitcom character hates their job? Whose lives are boring and unfulfilling? If you don't see yourself reflected on TV, society is telling you that *you don't exist*. Fake archetypes on TV find their way into real people.

Procrastination has seized the nation. Every moment slips away, leaving barely a trace in its wake. We can't always see where we're going, but let's get there. "A journey of a thousand miles begins with a single step." —*Lao Tzu, Tao Te Ching*

Do *you* feel represented by your government? It's tough to justify the taxes we pay them, given their poor results, without massive ignorance of the policies they support. The true check and balance to government madness is popular resistance.

Weird slime in every river, toxic genes in food. Natural resources aren't like other assets; their value just can't be measured on a spreadsheet. There is environmental destruction stored up in virtually every product made, and it adds up.

Nothing gets into our heads and souls like music. How do musicians get us to learn their lyrics? Music manages to install lyrical recall on a consistent and often permanent basis. Add guitar to your poetry and it resonates deeper.

Mental cloning has been practiced for ages. Ancient priests figured out that the limits of our perception could be framed as a battle between "good" and "evil." Political strategists have adopted this framework to great (and devastating) effect.

World War III is all around us - a network of murder with diverse actors working off the same script. Factories work overtime to meet the endless demand for these tools of military terror. Civilians pay the price for decades afterwards.

Our social universe is built on words, images, and the rituals and institutions and behaviors that derive from them. These forces are the realm of the artist, not the conqueror. The observer literally creates the world she observes.

"...the 'War Against Some Drugs' in America and elsewhere too is turning local police forces into armed occupiers, kicking down doors, killing innocent people, and not stopping the illicit drug trade whatsoever." —*Preston Peet*
http://www.disinfo.com/archive/pages/dossier/id203/pg1/

An army of clerics, TV news talking heads, political strategists and corporate PR flacks have conspired to keep workers in the dark. Protective laws gather dust as abuses continue and the poor are a constant reminder: "Back to work, you!"

The internal combustion engine is a KARMA MACHINE. Those bills are going to come due at some point; what is our civilization going to do when the sea level rises and the air turns toxic? I have an idea: let's turn it around now!

Time is meaningless to a person in the grip of an idea whose time for expression has come; rings of potential seem to radiate from one's pen, circling out towards the endless unknown frontier of poetry and personal power.

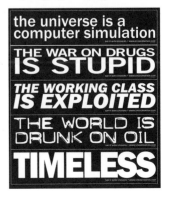

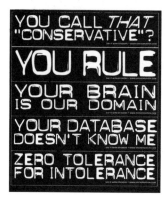

"Working in partnership, men and women together can make enormous strides toward changing attitudes and perceptions around domestic violence, sexual assault, and stalking." —*The US Department of Justice*
http://www.usdoj.gov/ovw/ovw_ad.htm

We are immersed in scenarios that are archetypal; that is, they resemble scenarios that many other people have had to navigate. These scenarios can be created, manipulated, and ended through psychological tactics, and they often are.

Some historians believe that the systematic use of lead for plumbing, cooking, and making wine was a cause of the Fall of the Roman Empire. This civilization seems determined to follow suit, seeing as they never show pollution on TV.

You can't pay the bills with "potential" and "momentum." Most of us have to find employment at some point, and "in a free market, you're on the price list." —*The Gang Of Four, "Return The Gift"*

It's almost as if the relationship of words and human beings was biological in nature. Language has, after all, evolved along with humankind, as has the technology for its reproduction. Words are written not for today but for *tomorrow*.

Innovation is simple. It's simply the process of wanting something to exist, seeing it doesn't, and making it yourself. Note that the verb "to *want*" is a critical part of that decision. Innovation is an inevitable result of the fire within you.

I may read a book of great ideas, but I'm not going to memorize a chapter; at most I jot down a few quotes. In contrast I have entire ALBUMS of rock lyrics down pat. I can barely quote Shakespeare but I have six Minutemen records in my head.

Ink may take ages to fade. The effects a given block of text has upon a reader, however, is never the same twice. The last time you read your favorite book, you got one thing out of it; the next time you'll get something else.

Our biases gently distort consensus reality to make it compatible with our experiences and attitudes. If we're destined to be subjective why not choose to believe in yourself? Express confidence in your capabilities and you'll wind up capable.

Only recently have people been able to publish without impressing someone who owns a printing press. The information environment is as polluted as the ecosystem, but people still assume they're informed about their beliefs.

What is it about the conservative end of the political spectrum that repels reality? Conservatives are wedded to an ideological battle against any aspect of *good* the government claims to provide the public. They are really *ANARCHISTS*.

My aim in writing this book is to help you. These stickers are like a Tarot deck; there's a blend of perspectives that you'll encounter at random and maybe they'll be catalysts for thinking differently about your situation. Hope it works!

I don't consider a creative effort "done" until I get feedback from those who check it out. Art is a "call and response" affair - you send energy out into the social universe, and you hear the echoes of your thoughts reverberate back.

Some of the smartest minds in recent history have joined the advertising industry and are using technology to segment society into demographics. They operate on the principle that your postal code determines who you are. Real smart.

We have the technology to become an antidote to the hemlock of political apathy and cultural submission. Systematic intolerance violates basic human rights. We see it all around us; it's time to take a stand.

StickerNation.com is a great way to get messages out into the world. If you are interested in printing up your own ideas on stickers, visit us at

www.StickerNation.com

You can get 250 copies of your message on custom vinyl stickers for just $50, which is an awesome deal. Your stickers will be 9 inches (229 mm) wide (longer than the ones in this book) and they'll be real vinyl, suitable for outdoor use. In addition we sell larger vinyl versions of all of the stickers in this book on our site for a dollar, so if one of these messages belongs on your car or bike, click on down!

—Srini
stickernation@gmail.com